The Path

#909

Nimatullahi Sufi Order

North America

306 West 11th Street
New York, New York 10014
U.S.A.
Tel: 212-924-7739

4931 MacArthur Blvd. NW
Washington, D.C. 20007
U.S.A.
Tel: 202-338-4757

84 Pembroke Street
Boston, Massachusetts 02118
U.S.A.
Tel: 617-536-0076

4021 19th Avenue
San Francisco, California 94132
U.S.A.
Tel: 415-586-1313

11019 Arleta Avenue
Mission Hills, Los Angeles,
California 91345, U.S.A.
Tel: 818-365-2226

219 Chace Street
Santa Cruz, California 95060
U.S.A.
Tel: 831-425-8454

310 NE 57th Street
Seattle, Washington 98105
U.S.A.
Tel: 206-527-5018

4642 North Hermitage
Chicago, Illinois 60640
U.S.A.
Tel: 773-561-1616

405 Greg Avenue
Santa Fe, New Mexico 87501
U.S.A.
Tel: 505-983-8500

3018 Felicita Road-Escondido
San Diego, California 92029
U.S.A.
Tel: 760-489-7834

1596 Ouest avenue des Pins
Montreal, Quebec H3G 1B4
Canada
Tel: 514-989-1411

1784 Lawrence Avenue West
North York, Toronto
Ontario M6L 1E2, Canada
Tel: 416-242-9397

1735 Mathers Avenue
West Vancouver
B.C. V7V 2G6, Canada
Tel: 604-913-1144

Europe

41 Chepstow Place
London W2 4TS
England
Tel: 020-7229-0769

95 Old Lansdowne Road
West Didsbury, Manchester
M20 2NZ, England
Tel: 0161-434-8857

Kölnerstraße 176
51149 Köln
Germany
Tel: 49 220-315-390

50 rue du Quatrième Zouaves
Rosny-sous-Bois 93110
Paris, France
Tel: 331-485-52809

116, avenue Charles de Gaulle
69160 Tassin-La-Demi-Lune
Lyon, France
Tel: 478-342-016

C/Abedul 11
Madrid 28036
Spain
Tel: 3491-350-2086

Cabezas, 9
14003 Córdoba
Spain
Tel: 957-48-43-91

Ringvägen 5
17276 Sundbyberg
Sweden
Tel: 46-8983-767

Jan van Goyenkade 19
2311 BA, Leiden
The Netherlands
Tel: 31-71-5124001

Getreidemarkt 3 /1A-1060
Wien, Austria
Tel: 431-9414022

Number II, House 4
Building 1A, Devyatkin Pereulok
Moscow, Russia
Tel: 7095-9247000

House 4, Building 43-H
1-2 Floors, Kapitanskaya Street
St. Petersburg, Russia
Tel: 921-0906611

Africa

63 Boulevard Latrille
BP 1224 Abidjan
CIDEX , 1 Côte d'Ivoire
Tel: 225-22410510

Quartier Beaurivage
BP 1599 Porto-Novo, Bénin
Tel: 229-20-214706

Quartier Guema
02 BP 86
Parakou, Bénin

Azimmo Secteur 16
Villa 12, Ouaga 2000
10 BP 356
Ouagadougou, Burkina Faso
Tel: 226-50-385797

Magnambougou Faso-Kanu
BP 2916
Rue 35, Porte 202
Bamako, Mali
Tel: 223-272-03-27

Australia

87A Mullens Street
Balmain 2041,
Sydney, Australia
Tel: 612-9555-7546

In the Name of the
Most Exalted and Transcendent

Also available by Dr. Javad Nurbakhsh:

Masters of the Path
Sufi Women
Divani Nurbakhsh: Sufi Poetry
Jesus in the Eyes of the Sufis
Spiritual Poverty in Sufism
The Great Satan, "Eblis"
Discourses on the Sufi Path
Dogs from a Sufi Point of View
The Psychology of Sufism
The Truths of Love: Sufi Poetry
Traditions of the Prophet, Vol. I
Traditions of the Prophet, Vol. II
Sufism I: Meaning, Knowledge and Unity
Sufism II: Fear and Hope, Contraction and Expansion, Gathering and Dispersion, Intoxication and Sobriety, Annihilation and Subsistence
Sufism III: Submission, Contentment, Absence, Presence, Intimacy, Awe, Tranquillity, Serenity, Fluctuation, Stability
Sufism IV: Repentance, Abstinence, Renunciation, Wariness, Humility, Humbleness, Sincerity, Constancy, Courtesy
Sufism V: Gratitude, Patience, Trust-in-God, Aspiration, Veracity, Zeal, Valour, Altruism, Shame
Sufi Symbolism I: Parts of the Beloved's Body; and Wine, Music, Audition and Convivial Gatherings
Sufi Symbolism II: Love, Lover, Beloved, Allusions and Metaphors
Sufi Symbolism III: Religious Terminology
Sufi Symbolism IV: Symbolism of the Natural World
Sufi Symbolism V: Veils and Clothing, Government, Economics and Commerce, Medicine and Healing
Sufi Symbolism VI: Titles and Epithets
Sufi Symbolism VII: Contemplative Disciplines, Visions and Theophanies, Family Relationships, Servants of God, Names of Sufi Orders
Sufi Symbloism VIII: Inspirations, Revelations, Lights, Charismatic Powers, Spiritual States and Stations, Praise and Condemnation
Sufi Symbolism IX: Spiritual Faculties, Spiritual Organs, Knowledge, Gnosis, Wisdom and Perfection
Sufi Symbolism X: Spiritual States and Mystical Stations
Sufi Symbolism XI: Spiritual States and Mystical Stations
Sufi Symbolism XII: Spiritual States and Mystical Stations
Sufi Symbolism XIII: Scribes, Pens, Tablets, Koranic Letters, Words, Discourse, Speech, Divine Names, Attributes and Essence
Sufi Symbolism XIV: The Unity of Being
Sufi Symbolism XV: Reality, the Divine Attributes and the Sufi Path
Sufi Symbolism XVI: Index

The Path

Sufi Practices

Dr. Javad Nurbakhsh

KHANIQAHI NIMATULLAHI PUBLICATIONS

NEW YORK LONDON

Published by Khaniqahi Nimatullahi Publications
U.K.: 41 Chepstow PLace, London W2 4TS
U.S.A.: 306 West 11th Street, New York, N.Y. 10014
www.nimatullahi.org

Library of Congress Cataloging-in Publication Data

Nurbakhsh, Javad.

[Dar kharābāt. English]

The Path: Sufi Practices/Javad Nurbakhsh.
p. cm.
Includes bibliographical references.
ISBN 0-933546-70-X (pbk.: alk. paper)

1. Sufism. 2. Sufism-Rituals. 3. Islam-Customs and practices.
I. Nurbakhsh, Javad. Dar bihisht-i ṣūfīyān. English.
II. Title.
BP189.5 .N8813 2002
297.4'4-dc21
2002013082

ISBN-13: 978-0-933546-70-7
Second printing, with revisions, 2006
Printed in the United States of America

Cover Design by James Killough
Book Design by Lolo Saney
Illustrations by Doug Gilbert

Khaniqah Nimatullahi Boston

84 Pembroke Street

Boston, MA 02118

Tel: (617) 536-0076

Email: Nimatullahisufiorder@gmail.com

Thursday at 6PM

• Saturday at 10:00 AM

• 5:00 PM

Name: ....

Address: ....

....

Email: ....

Tel: ....

Comments:

عشق

Contents

TRANSLITERATION EQUIVALENTS

CONSONANTS

PERSIAN ARABIC	LATIN	PERSIAN ARABIC	LATIN
ء	ʾ	ض	ḍ
ب	b	ط	ṭ
ت	t	ظ	ẓ
ث	th	ع	ʿ
ج	j	غ	gh
ح	ḥ	ف	f
خ	kh	ق	q
د	d	ك	k
ذ	dh	ل	l
ر	r	م	m
ز	z	ن	n
س	s	و	w
ش	sh	ه	h
ص	ṣ	ي	y
		ة	a

PERSIAN ARABIC	LATIN
LONG VOWELS	
آ	ā
أو	ū
اِي	ī
SHORT VOWELS	
َ	a
ُ	u
ِ	i
DIPTHONGS	
اَو	aw
اَي	ay
PERSIAN CONSONANTS	
پ	p
ژ	zh
چ	ch
گ	g

Introduction[1]

The substance and meaning of Sufism: the substance of Sufism is the Truth and the meaning of Sufism is the selfless experiencing and actualization of the Truth.

The practice of Sufism: the practice of Sufism is the intention to go towards the Truth by means of love and devotion. This is called the *ṭarīqat*, the spiritual path or way towards God.

The definition of the sufi: the sufi is one who is a lover of the Truth, who by means of love and devotion moves towards the Truth, towards the perfection that all are truly seeking. As necessitated by love's jealousy, the sufi is taken away from everything except the Truth. For this reason, in Sufism it is said that, "Those who are inclined towards the hereafter cannot pay attention to the material world. Likewise, those who are involved in the material world cannot concern themselves with the hereafter. But the sufi (because of love's jealousy) is unable to attend to either of these worlds."

Concerning this same idea, Shiblī has said, "One who dies for the love of the material world dies a hypocrite. One who dies for the love of the hereafter dies an ascetic. But one who dies for the love of the Truth dies a sufi."

Sufism

Sufism is a path for the actualization of divine ethics. It involves an enlightened inner being, not intellectual proof; revelation and witnessing, not logic. By divine ethics, we are referring to ethics that transcend mere social convention, a way of being that is the actualization of the attributes of God.

To explain the Truth is indeed a difficult task. Words, being limited, can never really express the perfection of the Absolute, the Unbound. Thus, for those who are imperfect, words create doubt and misunderstanding. Yet:

If one cannot drink up the entire ocean,
at least one can drink to one's limit.

Philosophers have written volumes and spoken endlessly about the Truth, but somehow their efforts have always fallen short. For the sufi, philosophers are those who view the perfection of the Absolute from a limited perspective; thus, all they see is part of the Absolute, not the Infinite in its entirety. What philosophers see may be correct, but it is only a part of the whole.

One is reminded of Rūmī's well-known story of a group of people in India who had never seen an elephant. One day they came to a place where there was an elephant. In complete darkness they approached the animal, each person touching it. Afterwards, they described what they thought they had perceived. Of course their descriptions were different. The one who had felt a leg, imagined the elephant to be a pillar. The one who felt the animal's ear described the elephant as a fan, and so on. Each one of their descriptions, with respect to the various parts they had experienced, was true. Yet, as far as accurately describing the whole, their conceptions had all fallen short. If they had possessed a candle, they would not have had different opinions. The candle's light would have revealed the elephant as a whole.

Only by the light of the spiritual path and the mystic way can the Truth be discovered. In order for one to truly witness the perfection of the Absolute, one must see with one's inner being, which perceives the whole of Reality. This witnessing happens only when one becomes perfect, losing one's (partial) existence in the Whole.

If the Whole is likened to the Ocean and one's existence to a drop, the sufi says that witnessing the Ocean with the eye of a drop is impossible. Only when the drop becomes one with the Ocean will it see the Ocean with the eye of the Ocean.

How Is It Possible to Realize Perfection?

Human beings are dominated by the self's desires and fears. Those who are ensnared in these habitual impulses are out of harmony with the Divine Nature, and thus are ill. As a result of this illness, feelings become disturbed and, accordingly, thoughts and perceptions become unsound. Thus, one's faith as well as one's knowledge of the Truth strays from what is Real.

To follow the way to perfection, these incorrect thought processes must first be rectified and these desires and fears transmuted. This can only be accomplished by coming into harmony with the Divine Nature. The way of harmony (the spiritual path) consists of spiritual poverty, devotion, and the continuous, selfless remembrance of God. In this way, one will come to perceive the Truth as it really is.

Asceticism and Abstinence in Sufism

To travel the path, the sufi needs strength supplied by proper bodily nourishment. It has been said that whatever the sufi eats is transformed into spiritual qualities and light. However, the food of others, since it but serves their own desires and fears, only strengthens their selfish attachments and takes them further from the Truth:

This one eats and only
stinginess and envy result,
While that one eats and there is but
the light of the One.
This one eats and only
impurity comes about,
While that one eats and all becomes
the light of God.

—Rūmī

It is clear that Sufism is not based upon ascetic practices such as abstinence from food. In our school, travelers of God's way are only instructed to abstain from food when they are sick or entangled in excessive desire or fear. In this case, the master or spiritual guide permits one to refrain from eating for a brief period of time and instead directs one to concentrate on spiritual practices. In this way the excess is transmuted and the seeker's inner being becomes harmonious. Then, the darvish will be able to continue on the dangerous ascent to the Infinite.

Some have thought that by fasting the strength necessary for purification is attained. On the contrary, in Sufism abstinence alone is not enough to purify the self. It is true that asceticism and abstinence may give one a certain spiritual state and that, in this state, one's perception may be clarified. But if the self is likened to a dragon that by fasting becomes powerless, it is certain that when the fast is broken and enough food is eaten, the dragon will revive and, stronger than ever, go about attempting to fulfill its desires.

In Sufism, it is by the *ṭarīqat* (spiritual path) that the self is gradually purified and its attributes transformed into Divine Attributes, until there is nothing left of one's 'commanding self'. In such extensive and precise work, asceticism and abstinence are virtually worthless.

The Spiritual Path

The *ṭarīqat* is the way by which the sufi comes into harmony with the Divine Nature. As we have said, this way is comprised of spiritual poverty (*faqr*), devotion and the continuous, selfless remembrance of God (*dhikr*), which are represented by the cloak of the darvish (*khirqa*).

1. Spiritual Poverty (*faqr*)

The feeling of seeking (*ṭalab*) is a manifestation of what is known in Sufism as spiritual poverty. This is the feeling of being imperfect and needy, along with the desire for perfection. Those in this state feel 'empty-handed', that they lack the higher attributes which are humanity's true potential. The Prophet Muḥammad has said in this regard, "My honor is from spiritual poverty. I have been honored over and above all prophets by being graced with spiritual poverty." And God revealed to the Prophet, "Say, God increase my true knowledge of You." As this saying indicates, even though Muḥammad was given the honor of prophethood, it was still necessary that he feel his poverty and desire to be nearer to the essence of God.

2. The Cloak of the Darvish (*Khirqa*) and Devotion

The *khirqa* is the darvish's garment of honor. It symbolizes the Divine Nature and Attributes. Some have mistakenly imagined that the cloak actually possesses these properties and that, if one were to wear such a cloak, one would become a saint. However, wearing spiritual clothing does not make one spiritual.

A sufi wears whatever he or she likes while being in harmony with what is socially approved. ʻAlī said, "Wear those clothes that neither cause you to be looked down upon nor admired and envied." Thus, it is not the clothes that make the sufi; rather, it is the sufi's actions and inner being.

Recline on the throne of the heart,
and with purity in manner be a sufi.

—Saʻdī

The cloak of the darvish is sewn with the needle of devotion and the thread of the selfless remembrance of God. The one who wishes to be honored by this cloak of poverty must, with devotion, surrender to a spiritual guide. True devotion draws one's heart towards the Beloved. It involves continuous attention to the Truth and constant effort to let go of attention to the self. This includes unquestioned obedience to one's spiritual guide.

The guide, by spiritual means, penetrates to the depths of the disciple's soul, transmutes his or her negative qualities, and brings to nothing the impurities of the world of multiplicity. In other words, the guide takes the needle of devotion from the disciple's hand and, with the thread of the disciple's selfless remembrance of God, sews the sufi cloak upon the disciple. Then, by the grace of this cloak of Divine Names and Attributes, the disciple will become a perfected being.

3. Continuous, Selfless Remembrance of God (*Dhikr*)

Contained in Absolute, Infinite Unity are forces that emanate and become manifested as created beings. Each being, according to its nature, receives grace from these forces. In the realm of words, the manifestations of these forces, or truths, are expressed by Divine Names. Two examples are: the Living (*al-Ḥayy*), meaning the life of creation is directly connected with God, and the Transcendent (*al-ʻAlī*), meaning the force of the universe is with God.

The Divine Names, in the continuous, selfless remembrance of God (*dhikr*), are prescribed by the master of the spiritual path to cure disciples of the disease of the self and its desires and fears. But this remembrance is of no value unless all of one's senses come to be fully centered on the meaning-reality of the respective Names. It is only by full acknowledgment and love of the reality of these Divine Names that attention to the self falls away. Then, the self becomes purified and adorned by the Divine Attributes:

For so long did the Beloved
face my open heart
That except for His Attributes and Nature
nothing remained of that heart.

—Maghribī

Only in such a fashion can the repetition of the Divine Names be called the selfless remembrance of God, or *dhikr*.

The disciple is like a machine whose energy comes from devotion. This machine, by means of the selfless remembrance of God, transmutes all of the self's desires and fears into Divine Attributes. Gradually, even the disciple's self passes away and the Divine Nature becomes manifest; then the disciple truly becomes the recipient of the sufi cloak, and the heart and soul become illuminated by the grace of the Divine Attributes. At this point the disciple is worthy of entering the spiritual feast of the sufis which takes place in the 'Tavern of Ruin' (*kharābāt*). This is the spiritual state of 'passing away of the self in God' (*fanā'*). Here, the sufi directly perceives the secrets of the Truth. As is said in the Koran, "Only the purified experience It (the Truth)" (56:79). These purified ones, in Sufism, are called Perfect Human Beings.

To show how the remembrance (*dhikr*) is done, let us take the example of *lā ilāha ill Allāh* ('there is no god, but God'). The sufi sits either cross-legged or on the heels, with the right hand placed on the left thigh and the left hand over the right wrist. In these positions one's hands and legs form a *lā* (the negative particle in Arabic), symbolizing the nonexistence of the sufi before the Beloved. In this state, the sufi must relinquish attention to and belief in this world, the hereafter, and oneself.

The *lā* of one's arms begins at the navel and continues up to the neck. This forms a scissors that symbolizes the cutting away of the head of the self and the surrendering of the belief in and attachment to one's own limited existence.

With *ilāha*, the sufi moves the head and neck toward the right in a semicircle. This is called the arc of possible existence. The movement symbolizes the negation, or rather the giving up, of the belief in the reality of 'other than God'. 'Other than God' in Sufism is all transient, limited and possible existences. Human beings attend to these possible existences instead of the Eternal, All-encompassing, Necessary and Absolute Reality of God.

Then, with *ill Allāh*, the sufi moves the head and neck to the left. This is called the arc of necessity and symbolizes the reality of the Necessary, Absolute Reality.

The Manifestation of the Divine

Since words are the manifestations of objects, concepts and truths, sufis feel that by continuous and complete attention to the meaning and reality of the remembrance of God, they become the true manifestations of that remembrance. That is to say, with continuous, selfless remembrance of a Divine Name, a Divine Attribute comes to predominate in the sufi's being.

The sufis consider that there is a particular Divine Attribute that dominates the being of every prophet and saint, such that each can be said to be the incarnation of that Attribute. For example, sufis feel that Moses is the manifestation of the transcendent aspect of Reality because of his ability to speak with God without an intermediary. In the Koran, the Lord said to Moses, "Do not fear, because you are transcendent." Jesus is the manifestation of prophethood. While an infant he cried, "God gave me the book and placed me as a prophet."

All of the prophets are manifestations of the Divine Unity and Perfection, but Muḥammad is its supreme manifestation. His name is the most exalted of the Divine Names, containing all the Names within it. That is, Muḥammad is the spiritual incarnation and manifestation of all of God's Names. As Muḥammad has said, "What God first created was my light."

In addition, each prophet is the manifestation of one of the Divine Attributes, and all of the Attributes are contained in the most exalted Name. Also, Muḥammad is the manifestation of the Great Name. So, due to the fact that his manifestation is inclusive of all the Names, he hierarchically comes before all other created things, and for the same reason said, "I was a prophet while Adam was still between water and earth."

Samā'

If you are not one with the Beloved,
Seek!

And if you are in Union,
Rejoice!

—Rūmī

The musical and ecstatic aspect of Sufism is called *samā'*. The sufis, while being spiritually enraptured, give all the attention of their hearts to the Beloved. While listening to special and rhythmical music, and sometimes with prescribed movements, they engage in the selfless remembrance of God. In this state, the sufis are drunken lovers who lose awareness of everything but God. With all their faculties, the sufis are attentive to the Beloved and have totally given up and forgotten themselves.

Not all disciples engage in *samā'*. It is only given as a practice to some by their spiritual guide, who determines whether it is appropriate for them or not. *Samā'* may be likened to a medicine: it is sometimes prescribed and sometimes prohibited.

Sainthood

Earlier, we have said that the aim of Sufism is the cultivation of Perfect Human Beings who are mirrors reflecting the Divine Names and the Divine Attributes. In Sufism, a perfected being is also called a *walī* (saint), a word that literally means 'sincere friend'. All who have been prophets have also been saints. The spiritual degree of sainthood is a station indicating the condition of one's inner being, while the rank of prophethood reflects one's mission as a Divine messenger in the world.

The prophetic mission of Muḥammad was both Absolute Sainthood and Prophecy. 'Alī, while not among the prophets, attained to this same Absolute Sainthood. Muḥammad said, "'Alī and I are of the same light," and 'Alī said, "Spiritually, I have been with all the Prophets."

These perfected beings or saints, each according to his or her own capacity, have drunk from the fountain of Truth. Because they are known only by God, only God can truly know the differences among their spiritual stations. In a prophetic tradition (*ḥadīth*), God says, "My friends (saints) are under my banner; no one knows them but Me."

Most people do not have the patience necessary to know the saints. Those who are encompassed cannot truly know what encompasses them. True knowledge of the saints comes from knowing their reality through one's inner being.

A common misunderstanding is the idea that by going into seclusion one can become a saint. However, in the way of the sufi, one must live in society. Being a recluse and retreating from contact with people has no lasting spiritual value.

Muḥammad said, "The faith of a believer is not perfect unless one thousand sincere people give witness to his 'infidelity'." He meant that the Divine Knowledge of a perfect believer is beyond the level of most people's thinking. Thus, those who hear such a perfected being speak, since they cannot perceive the truth of what is being said, will call him or her an unbeliever.

A true believer, a sufi, must live in, serve and guide society and be a vehicle by which society receives God's Grace. It is for this reason that conforming to and being in harmony with society, being at peace with all, is one of the qualities of a perfected being.

Purification and Its Stages

The stages of purification are:

1. self becoming empty.
2. self becoming illuminated.
3. self becoming adorned.
4. self having passed away *(fanā')*.

These stages occur in the course of the selfless remembrance of God (*dhikr*). The first stage, becoming emptied, entails letting go of the negative qualities, the desires which originate from the self. The second stage of becoming illuminated involves polishing the heart and soul of the tarnish of belief in, and attachment to, the self. In the third stage, one's inner being becomes adorned by Divine Attributes. Ultimately, the being of the disciple becomes completely filled by the Attributes of the Truth, to the extent that there is no sign of his or her own limited existence. This fourth stage is called 'self having passed away' *(fanā')*.

I thought of You so often that
I completely became You.
Little by little You drew near,
and slowly but slowly I passed away.

The disciple, through these stages of purification, travels the inner way, the spiritual path (*ṭarīqat*). Having traveled this path, the disciple becomes a perfected being and arrives at the threshold of the Truth (*ḥaqīqat*). Muḥammad said, "The *sharī'at* is my speech, the *ṭarīqat* my actions, and the *ḥaqīqat* my states."

One could liken the journey within the *ḥaqīqat*, the Truth, to training in a Divine university, known in Sufism as the 'Tavern of Ruin' (*kharābāt*). In this true center for higher education there are no professors, one's only guide being Absolute Love. Here one's only teacher is love, one's books are love, and one's being is love.

Before a perfected being enters this university, he or she can be defined. Upon entering the Truth, however, one is indefinable, beyond the realm of mere words.

Footprints but come to the Ocean's shore.
Therein, no trace remains.

—Rūmī

If you ask his name, like Bāyazīd he answers, "I lost him years ago. The more I seek him, the less I find." If you ask of his religion, like Rūmī, he answers:

The way of a lover is not among the religions;
The church and state of lovers is God.

If you ask who he is, like Bāyazīd he answers, "There is nothing under my cloak but Allāh." If he speaks, like Ḥallāj, you may hear him sing, "I am the Truth."

Such words can truly come only from perfected beings who have lost their 'selves' and become the manifestation of the Divine Nature and Divine Mysteries. Their selves have departed and only God remains.

[1] This essay was originally delivered as a speech at the Sorbonne University in 1963 (at the invitation of Henry Corbin).

The Aim[1]

The Definition of Sufism

Sufism is a school of spiritual states, not discourse, and a sufi is something to become, not something to merely read about. Since spiritual states cannot be expressed in words, sufi shaikhs have declared, "Whatever can be expressed in words is not Sufism." As Rūmī has stated:

> *When I come to love, I am ashamed*
> *of all that I have ever said about love.*

Whatever great sufis have said in explanation of Sufism (*taṣawwuf*) was the result of and appropriate to their particular situations and states. Such explanations, therefore, do not constitute general definitions of Sufism. Rather, they refer to some of its characteristics. What can be considered, to some extent, a general definition of Sufism is this:

> Sufism is a path towards the Truth where there are no provisions except love. Its method is to look solely in one direction, and its objective is God. That is, at the end of the path nothing remains but God.

The Aim of Sufism

The aim of Sufism is the realization of the Truth. Although philosophers believe that such an aim can be achieved using reason and a process of logic or argument, the realization of the Truth is truly possible only with the eye of the heart and the conscience, through a process of unveiling and illumination. Thus, Sufism means going and seeing, not sitting and talking.

Who is the Sufi?

The sufi is one who moves toward the Truth by means of love and devotion. He or she knows that the realization of the Truth is only possible for the Perfect Human Being, or the Perfected One, for in a state of imperfection human beings are unable to recognize the Truth. Imperfection can be seen as an abnormal condition in which one's ability to see things as they really are is deficient. Imperfect beings, by virtue of their imperfection, misperceive the Truth without being aware of it, and therefore their understanding of the Truth is unconsciously mistaken.

In the view of the sufis, what is known as the 'commanding self' (*nafs-i 'ammāra*), which resides in the unconscious, closely monitors and dominates the thoughts and behavior of each individual. Consequently, one's ability to discriminate is clouded by the desires and attachments of this 'commanding self' and discrimination is necessarily faulty.

Sufiologists

Those who study Sufism and derive their own interpretations are called *mutaṣawwifa*, or 'sufiologists'. Although such people may possess a great deal of information about sufi characteristics, they do not really know the sufis. They do not have sufi characteristics themselves, nor can they know what the sufi sees with the eye of the heart. Therefore, their statements about Sufism will probably not be authoritative for sufis, although they might be interesting from the point of view of defining or explaining Sufism.

Who is the Perfected One?

Since only one who is perfect is capable of realizing the Truth, sufis strive their utmost for perfection. For sufis, the model and manifestation of the Perfected One in the external world is 'Alī ibn Abī Ṭālib, the cousin of the Prophet of Islam. Also, all the sufi masters and shaikhs were beings who realized varying degrees of perfection.

The question arises here of why 'Alī, as a disciple of the Prophet, should be considered the model of the Perfected One, rather than the Prophet himself. Sufis do, indeed, believe that the Prophet is the manifestation of perfection. But the Prophet's perfection was a gift of God, whereas 'Alī achieved perfection and mastership through being a disciple of the Prophet. It is from the perspective of his discipleship that he provides the model for sufis.

Conceptually, the Perfected One is an individual who has become freed from the dictates of the 'commanding self'. Both inwardly and outwardly, such beings are the manifestation of Divine Attributes. Having become one with the Absolute, they are freed from the relativity of 'I' and 'we'. They are mirrors which perfectly reflect God. When one looks upon them, one sees nothing but the Truth.

Seeking

The attraction towards God, indeed, all movement forward on the path, is due to the Will of God alone, as expressed in the Koran where God tells the Prophet, "It is not you who are responsible for guiding them, for God guides whom He wills" (2:272). This attraction toward God is called *ṭalab*, which means both 'calling' from God's direction and 'seeking' from humanity's. *Ṭalab* is the force that aids and encourages disciples during their movement towards perfection. It generates in them a feeling of dissatisfaction with their present condition, compelling them to seek a state of peace.

Although this compulsion is God at work within the seeker, it is equally vital to have a master as the outward manifestation of God's Will.

The Disciple

The relationship between the master and the disciple pertains to the intermediate phase of the spiritual path. The goal of the spiritual path is for the self of the traveler to become transformed from the 'commanding self' (*nafs-i 'ammāra*), to the 'blaming or reproving self' (*nafs-i lawwāma*), and finally to the 'self at rest' (*nafs-i muṭma'ina*). The motivation of the 'commanding self' is to satisfy its animal instincts and desires. The 'reproving self' blames the 'commanding self' for this and seeks perfection. The 'self at rest' has found peace and come to perfection. At this point, the disciple is worthy of attending the banquet of Unity in the Divine Presence, as referred to in the Koranic verse, "O Self at Rest, return to your Lord, well-pleased, and well-pleasing" (89:28).

While traveling the path and observing its rules and manners (*ādāb*), disciples are freed from the pressures of psychological conflicts. They are cleansed of egotistical qualities, and the energy that was previously taken up in worldly distractions is now used to polish the heart and mind. At the end of the path, disciples are emptied of the attributes of the self and adorned by the Divine Attributes. Such beings have truly put into practice the saying of the Prophet, "Make yourself in harmony with Divine Nature."

In the initial stage of the path, disciples undergo a process of confirming their faith in the master and gaining assurance that the master can take them to the final aim of human perfection. During this phase, the master determines that the seeker has proceeded with sincerity and devotion and is deserving of his guidance.

Once the master and disciple have accepted each other, the master assures the disciple that all of his or her previous misbehavior will be forgiven provided that from then on the disciple does not engage in what has been prohibited. From the sufi point of view, the initiation into the *ṭarīqat* is a second birth for the disciple. As Jesus has said, "He who enters not into the angelic kingdom of the heavens and earth is one who has not been born again." Sufis believe that an initiated person is born twice: once from his or her mother and once again into the world of love, loving kindness, devotion and unity.

The initial phase of the path generally takes from seven to twelve years. In the words of Ḥāfiẓ:

The aim of shepherd Moses
of the Promised Land
was reached only after years of service
at master Shu'ayb's hand.

The Master

The master is a Perfected One who has at the very least completed all phases of the path. Being a master is not something merely to be claimed; it must be attained through training under another perfect master. The true master is linked to the spiritual chain of masters that extends back to the Prophet.

Traveling the path can be done in two ways:

> 1. By means of Divine Grace—wherein God seizes a devotee and takes that one away from himself or herself, bestowing His Presence. A person carried away in this manner is called *majdhūb*, or 'an enraptured one'. This, however, is a rare occurrence.
>
> 2. By means of discipleship—being a traveler (*sālik*) on the path. This is the way of striving, as expressed in the Koranic passage, "Those who strive toward Us, We shall certainly guide them in Our ways." (29:69)

One who has achieved the end in only one of these ways, as either *majdhūb* or *sālik* cannot be a master. A master must have gone from a state of 'enrapturement' (*jadhba*) to that of 'traveling' (*sulūk*), or the reverse. Neither state alone is perfection, and the master must be perfect.

In short, the masters must have traveled the path and come to know the path before they can lead others on the way.

The Rules and Manners of Discipleship

The true disciple is one who witnesses in the heart the spiritual beauty of the master and immediately falls in love with this beauty. Being such a lover is the source of all blessings. Until the disciple has fallen in love with the Divine Beauty of the master, he or she cannot surrender to the master's will. In truth, the disciple is one who surrenders to the master's will, not one who remains the disciple of his or her own will.

O heart, if you want the Beloved to be content,
do and say whatever He desires.
If He says cry tears of blood, don't ask why;
and if He says give up your soul, don't ask the reason.

The first step then, after choosing a master and becoming inspired with faith in him or her, is to obey the master's instructions without questioning 'how' or 'why'.

On the way to the Beloved Laylā's abode,
there are many dangers and risks.
Unless you are an insane lover like Majnūn,
don't take even a single step.

Whatever the master orders, even if it is not immediately clear to the disciple, should be carried out. As Ḥāfiẓ has said:

Stain your prayer rug with wine
if the Master of the Holy Fire so commands.

The same point is illustrated in the Koranic story of Moses and Khiḍr in which Moses asks Khiḍr (the master of the path) for permission to become his disciple and is told, "If thou followest me, ask me about nothing until I myself mention it to you" (18:70).

The disciple should never try to challenge the master in any pursuit. It is in reference to this that it has been said, "love is but an Ethic," to which may be added "...and the path is merely observance of that Ethic."

The Course of the Path

The disciple's development falls into two stages. In the first, he or she undergoes a process of resolving psychological conflicts and lessening the control of the self until reaching a state of psychological harmony, equilibrium and peace of mind. In the second, the disciple undergoes a process of becoming illuminated by the Divine Attributes and Divine Nature.

From the viewpoint of modern psychotherapy, during the initial stage of the path, the master observes and studies the behavior of the disciple. In this process, as in psychotherapy, the interpretation of dreams and visions plays an important role. Disciples relate their dreams and visions to the master, who, understanding their meaning and significance, perceives the disciples' inner conflicts and compulsions and undertakes to cure them. It is important here that disciples refrain from speaking about their dreams and visions to anyone other than the master.

In this way, the first stage of the path is properly psychotherapeutic, varying in length according to the individual's own particular psychological condition. Modern psychotherapy is, in fact, an imperfect imitation of the sufi approach since it lacks spiritual content. Moreover, the curative process of Sufism results in the purification not only of the mind, but of the heart. With the elixir of love, the master liberates disciples from self-centered qualities and opens them to the manifestation of Divine Attributes.

In the beginning of the path, disciples should adhere to the following instructions:

1. Observance of Islam.
2. Cultivation of kindness to God's creatures.
3. Maintenance of discretion concerning the secrets of the path, both with respect to fellow darvishes and to outsiders.
4. Obedience to the rules of the path.

Once the master sees that the disciples are ready to undertake the process of the *ṭarīqat*, he or she inculcates the *dhikr* in them.

Remembrance of the Divine Names

The *dhikr* of the sufis is a Name of God transmitted to the disciple in a special manner by the master of the path. Through the inculcation of *dhikr*, the master instructs the disciple how to be in continuous remembrance of the Divine.

When the disciple is continually involved with the remembrance of God, his or her being gradually becomes liberated from egotistical and selfish qualities and illuminated by the Divine Attributes and Divine Nature.

In the beginning, the purpose of remembering God is to create a 'unity of attention'. Until this is attained, the disciple will be attentive to the various attachments of the self. Therefore, one should try to incline one's scattered attention to the all-encompassing point of Unity.

The remembrance of God effaces the memory of all other things, and the energy that was previously dispersed in worthless and short-term concerns now finds its proper focus in the remembrance of God. At the same time, psychological conflicts are reduced, leading to peace of mind in the disciple.

In the course of remembrance, the sufi is attentive to the Name itself, as well as to its meaning or significance. This is necessary since human beings have the habit of being attentive to a concept by means of words. Thus, when a word is remembered, the corresponding concept tends to arise in one's awareness. Attention to the Name alone however is a kind of idol-worship, for the word itself has no special properties. Of course, in the beginning, the disciple has no alternative but to focus on the words of the remembrance, coming gradually to the association of form and meaning until he or she is able to dispense with the form of the words altogether.

I will pass away from word, utterance and act,
so without these three, I can be with You.

—Rūmī

Sufis believe that disciples in remembrance should not only forget this world and the hereafter, but themselves as well. As long as disciples are conscious of themselves in the course of remembrance, they are regarded as being in a state of infidelity.

The *dhikr* of the sufis, then, is like a flood that eventually eliminates the self-centered qualities and illuminates the Divine Attributes in the disciple's heart. Ultimately, the very illusion of 'self' also becomes swept away and taken by this flood. This marks the end of the path and the beginning of the Ocean of selflessness.

Yet the remembrance itself is not sufficient to achieve this end. Devotion to the master is what really brings about the aim. Until the sense of devotion has overwhelmed the disciple, the tree of *dhikr* cannot bring forth the fruit of *fanā'* ('passing away of the self in God').

The Divine Names and Attributes

Sufis believe that the Names of God have no limit—each Name representing an Attribute, each Attribute evoking an understanding, and each understanding effecting a realization of the Divine Omnipresence. The transcendent quality of each Attribute shines before the eyes of one who is devoted to God and brings peace upon that one according to his or her individual capacity. Each time an Attribute is revealed through a flash of light, through the window of a Divine Name, the disciple's ardor and longing increase.

Miracles and Powers

True sufis are not concerned at all with miracles and spiritual powers. They make no claim of being the source of miracles or of possessing powers beyond those that human beings normally possess. Since the sufi negates everything but God, he or she considers such claims to be manifestations of *being*, or affirmations of a separate existence apart from God. That is, the sufi regards the self as relative in relation to the absoluteness of God, and considers all acts and intuitions issuing from the self to be obstacles in receiving the grace of God.

Some people mistakenly imagine that sufi masters claim to possess spiritual powers or to perform miracles. However, sufi masters themselves make no such claims. Rather, it is disciples who, by virtue of their devotion, may see miraculous or spiritual powers in the master or shaikh. At certain stages, therefore, it may be necessary for the master to liberate the disciple from this idol-worshipping frame of mind and lead him or her back to awareness of God.

Free Will and Determinism

At the beginning of the path, according to sufis, free will (*tafwīḍ*) is the predominating factor since the disciple is still entangled in the conflicts of the self. At this point, the disciple is largely influenced by the dictates of the self's desires, which overwhelm the individual will. In accordance with the Koranic verse, "Man has naught but what he strives for" (53:39), one should apply one's own will in order to become emptied of the self's compulsions and to prepare oneself to fully manifest the Divine Attributes. This process can take place only through individual effort combined with Divine Attraction.

At the end of the disciple's traveling, with the 'passing away of individual action' (*fanā-yi af ʿāl*) and the illumination of Divine Attributes in the inner being, the disciple sees that everything is determined (*jabr*). Here, there is no more interposition of 'I' or 'we'; all that the sufi does or wills is that which God does or wills.

Solitude While in Society

Sufis consider idleness and laziness a disgrace, and concern themselves as much as possible with service to the society in which they live. In this way, they serve God's creation externally while within they are preoccupied with God alone. As Saʿdī has expressed:

Have you ever heard of one
who is absent and present at the same time?
'Tis I, who am in the crowd
while my heart has gone beyond.

The greatest discipline for the sufi is to live harmoniously among people. This is a sign of human perfection. In contrast, one who is unable to have such harmony is considered to be imperfect. In the view of the sufi, perfection can be attained only in society. It is in this regard that the expression 'inner journey and outward manner' has been used, indicating that the inner spiritual journey is not enough to take one to perfection. Perfection can be realized only when one's actions are in harmony with God's creation and one's inner being is focused solely upon God.

Sufis are not only kind and of service to others, but they are also not offended by the ego-oriented behavior of people. Society is the touchstone of perfection for sufis—whenever they become offended by others or act reproachfully towards behavior directed against them, they have fallen into infidelity. As Ḥāfiẓ has said:

We bear reproach with joy,
remaining faithful,
For taking offense at another's acts
is infidelity on the Beloved's way.

Those who are unfaithful in this manner are caught up in duality, for they perceive God and themselves as separate entities.

Fanā' and *Baqā'*

The end of the spiritual path, of traveling towards God, is the spiritual station (*maqām*) of *fanā'* ('passing away of the self in God').[2] There are two kinds of fanā'': outer and inner. The outer *fanā'* is the 'passing away of individual action' (*fanā-yi af 'āl*), with the resulting manifestation of Divine Action. Those who reach this station become drowned in the Ocean of Divine Action, so that they perceive in all events the Action and Will of God, seeing neither themselves nor any other individual as one who does or wills any event. They become so completely without will that no trace of willing any individual action remains in them.

The inner *fanā'* involves the 'passing away of the attributes of the self' (*fanā-yi ṣifat*) and the 'passing away of the essence of the self' (*fanā-yi dhāt*). Sometimes, in discovery of the Divine Attributes, the possessors of this state (*ḥāl*) become drowned in the passing away of their own attributes. At other times, in witnessing the exalted effects of the Divine Essence, they become drowned in the passing away of their essence.

In the beginning of this inner *fanā'*, sufis lose their senses. Gradually, according to their capacity, the condition of being both absent and present at the same time descends upon them. Inwardly they are drowned in the ocean of *fanā'*, while outwardly they participate in the events around them.

There are many examples of sufis experiencing this condition. It is reported that 'Alī was once struck in the leg by an arrow in the course of battle. His companions tried to remove it but failed because the arrow had penetrated so deeply. Asking the Prophet's advice, they were told to take out the arrow while 'Alī was in prayer, which they then did easily. In another account, the sufi Muslim ibn Yasār was praying in the congregational mosque of Baṣra when a supporting column collapsed. The sound it made was so loud that everyone in the bazaar outside heard it. Yet, ibn Yasār, in the mosque itself, was unaware of what had happened.

Baqā' is the beginning of the 'journey in God'. Having caused the passing away of the disciple's will, God endows such a slave with His Will, so that whatever the slave wills is now the Will of the Divine. This *baqā'* corresponds to the outer *fanā'*.

The *baqā'* corresponding to the inner *fanā'*, on the other hand, is one in which the very veils that are the temporary essence and attributes of the disciple's self are removed. Here, God neither veils the creation, nor does the creation veil God. The veil has been totally removed and duality transformed into Unity.

1 This essay was originally delivered as a speech at the American University in Beirut in 1967 during a conference on World Religions.

2 For the difference between 'station' (*maqām*) and 'state' (*ḥāl*), see this book, the chapter on Self-Examination, section on Sayings of the Greatest Sufis about Self-Examination.

The Steps

Those who believe, who have left their homes and striven with their wealth and their lives in God's way, are of much greater worth in God's sight. These are the ones who are triumphant.

—Koran 9:20

This verse was revealed to explain the war that is incumbent upon believers in the external world, that Truth might gain victory over falsehood (i.e. Islam over unbelief). Believers must leave their homes and not hesitate to surrender their wealth and lives.

But this is the lesser war. The greater war is the victory of Absolute Being over relative existence. In order to fulfill this task and reach the goal of the Truth, believers must leave behind the domain of the self, and pass beyond desire for both this world and the next.

Thus, as this verse explains, faith in God is not enough. What must be accomplished is the cutting away of the ego, the self; what must be done is to fly towards God. On such a path, believers must do all they can to surrender not only their wealth and lives, but their very selves.

The first step towards the Absolute is stepping on all that is other than the Absolute, by going beyond both this world and the next for God's sake. As the friend of God, Muḥammad, has said:

> This world is forbidden to the people of the next world, and the next world is forbidden to the people of this world, and both are forbidden to the people of God.

So also Shiblī has said:

> There are three sorts of death: dying for this world, dying for the hereafter, and dying in the way of the Lord. One who dies in love of this world is a hypocrite; one who dies in love of the hereafter is a devotee; but one who dies in love of the Lord is a sufi.

It is said that Bāyazīd was once walking along a road with his disciples when they came upon a severed head by the wayside. Upon its forehead was written, "He loseth both the world and the hereafter" (Koran 22:11). Bāyazīd picked up the head and kissed it. When his disciples asked who the man was, he answered, "This is the head of a darvish who gave up both worlds for God."

My father Adam sold Eden for two grains of wheat.
What sort of son am I if I do not sell it
for one grain of barley?

—Ḥāfiẓ

As Ḥāfiẓ explains here, if the father has lost Paradise for two grains of wheat (as in the Torah it says he lost it for an apple), then he as his descendent will sell heaven for a single grain of barley. There is a subtle point here: 'barley' (*jaw*) in the system of numerological equivalents equals nine; and the word 'nothing' (*hīch*) is also nine. Perhaps Ḥāfiẓ is declaring that he will trade the garden of paradise for nothing, for the sake of God. Sa'dī had the same intent when he said:

The Friend is enough for us,
you take all the bounties of paradise!

The second step towards the Absolute is stepping on one's very existence and forgetting oneself for God's sake. As Muḥammad has said, "Die before you die." That is to say, die voluntarily before you are forced to die out of necessity. Again, Ḥāfiẓ has said:

Between lover and Beloved there is no veil.
Ḥāfiẓ, you yourself are your own veil.
Rise from this 'between'.

As long as you remain 'you', it will be impossible to reach the Absolute, for you will never see God with the eye of this 'you-ness'. When 'you' are not, though, God is, God who sees Himself with His own Eye. The drop cannot see the ocean with the eye of a drop. It must first lose itself in the Ocean of Reality that it may see the Ocean with the eye of the Ocean. The relative cannot comprehend the Absolute. The part must join the Whole if it is to comprehend the Whole with absolute understanding.

It is said that when Ḥallāj met Ibrāhīm al-Khawwāṣ, Ḥallāj asked him what he had gained from his forty years on the sufi path. Ibrāhīm answered that he had made the doctrine of trust in God particularly his own. Ḥallāj then exclaimed, "O lose yourself! For then there'll be no need to trust in God."

It is also said that when Bāyazīd reached the station of Nearness, he heard a voice that ordered him, "Ask for something!"

"I have no desire," he replied. "You ask for something."

Again the command was repeated, "Ask for something!"

Bāyazīd answered, "I want only You."

The voice then said, "So long as even an atom of the existence of Bāyazīd remains, this is impossible."

Maghribī has said:

That spiritual Friend knocked at my door last night.
"Who is it?" I asked. He answered, "Open the door. It is you!"
"How can I be You?" I asked. He answered, "We are one,
but the veil has hidden us in duality."
We and I, he and you, have become the veil,
and how well this has veiled you from yourself!
If you wish to know how we and he and all are one,
pass beyond this 'I', this 'we', this 'you'.
Pass from this world with all its old and new,
and see that all its ancientness and novelty are one.
Paintings and pictures are paintings and pictures no doubt,
but the artist is hidden in the artist's art.
In this lovely melody, behold nothing but the Minstrel,

for every sweet strain you hear is played by Him.
O Maghribī! You are the shadow of the Sun of the Orient,
and, like a shadow, you run after the Sun!

God says in the Koran, "God will bring a people whom He loves and who love Him" (Koran 5:54). That is, the love of God for humanity precedes the love of humanity for God. As Maghribī has said:

No one by himself can find a way towards Him.
Whoever goes to His quarters walks on His feet.

Thus, God must love the slave before the slave can love God. This road will never be traveled without God's aid and grace. It is an abundant overflow that draws one—something that is given, not something to be acquired through learning. This end is simply a fortunate occurrence: God scatters the seeds of "those whom He loveth." With the guidance of a perfect master, the receptive earth of "those who love Him" is watered, and the verdant tree of human perfection, of "Return unto thy Lord, content in His good pleasure" (Koran 89:28), will raise its head to the sky of Unity. Ḥāfiẓ has said:

Though union with Him is never given
as a reward for one's efforts,
Strive, O heart, as much as you can!

For although not everyone who ran after the gazelle captured it, the one who captured it had to run after it!

Answers

Over the past few years, many American and European people have come to express an interest in Eastern culture and thought. This spirit of inquiry has led many to the study of Sufism. With increasing frequency, for example, I have been receiving letters from darvishes and others interested in Sufism containing questions about Islamic mysticism and the way to the Truth. Since the questions posed in these letters are profoundly interrelated, I have grouped them topically in this essay in order to provide answers that may offer some insight into the method and practice of Sufism.

Clearly, anyone desiring a deeper knowledge of theoretical mysticism should refer to the prose and poetry of the classical sufis. If God wishes, such people will eventually become seekers on the path to the Truth through practical Sufism. May God's grace be upon their seeking.

The Sufi Path

Citizens of every nation and believers of every religion follow their various paths with the intention of getting somewhere, gaining something, or becoming someone. The sufi path, however, leads to non-being, loss of self, and passing away in the Beloved. As Khwāja 'Abdullāh Anṣārī has said:

O God! Non-being is an affliction for all,

but a blessing for me.

Thus, whoever enters the path of love in order to achieve a spiritual station or 'high state of consciousness' has taken the first step wrongly. Rūmī, the great Persian poet and sufi, has told the following story in this regard:

> Once, a lover came to the Beloved's house. The lover knocked on the door. "Who is it?" the Beloved asked. The lover answered, "It is I, Your lover." "Go away," said the Beloved, "for you are not really in love." Years passed, and again the lover came to the door of the Beloved's house and knocked. "Who is it?" asked the Beloved. This time the lover answered, "It is You." "Now that you are I," replied the Beloved, "you may come in."

Thus, the sufi is one who goes on the path in order to not 'be'.

The Travels of the Sufis

Ordinary people travel from here to there concerned with worldly matters. Ascetics reject this world and look towards paradise, striving to journey to the hereafter. Sufis, however, abandon traveling altogether and let go of themselves in search of God:

I abandoned traveling and lived
with the Beloved. What bliss,
O God, have I received from
this kind of traveling!

—Rūmī

The gnostics (*ārif*) travel within themselves, whereas the sufis travel *from* themselves. The gnostics say, "Know thyself, in order to know God." The sufis say, "Let go of yourself, in order to be free." People of the world journey in the realm of existence; the sufis journey in the realm of non-existence. Those in the material world are forever in a mad rush, never at rest. Sufis, however, are content with their present state, whatever it is. They are serene and at peace.

Thus, the sufis travel from themselves toward God.

The Sufi's Occupation

Sufis spend all of their energy in the way of the Beloved. They know that using their energy in any other way is a waste. For this reason, the sufis' work is creative and serves society. In addition, sufis at work are thankful for whatever God provides. They carry out their responsibilities effectively and sincerely, with the highest possible efficiency, because they seek God's satisfaction and not their own.

In view of this, most sufi masters have engaged in a life occupation. On the sufi path, those who do not work and exist as parasites, living off society, cannot be true worshippers of God. As Muḥammad, the Prophet of God, has said:

> *Whoever does not have work*
> *does not have religion.*

Thus, the person without work is not a sufi.

The Service of the Sufi

Since sufis are in love with God, they seek to serve Him with complete sincerity. The best way to serve God is to serve people. In order to re-affirm their devotion to God, sufis endeavor wholeheartedly to serve all people. Moreover, they do so with no expectation of spiritual or material reward. They consider being able to serve as a blessing from God, and thus they render service to everyone humbly, with all their hearts and souls. As Sa'dī has said:

> *Worshipping God is not done with*
> *rosary beads, prayer carpet, or robe.*
> *Worshipping God is serving others.*

Some sufis, in the way of selfless devotion, have chosen arduous careers in order to perform service to society. Other sufis have sought to make friends with people of aggressive or distasteful dispositions, enduring without complaint the rigors of such an association. By guiding and uplifting these people, the sufi relieves society of their bad behavior and averts any harm they might inflict.

Thus, the sufi is a servant of all humanity.

The Sufi's Remembrance of God (*Dhikr*)

The sufi is a lover of God. Like one who is enraptured in human love, always thinking of his or her lover, the sufi's heart, ravished by Divine Love, is continually immersed in remembrance of the Divine Beloved:

Don't be inattentive to the Beloved,
not even for the blink of an eye;
For perhaps in that moment She'll look,
and you'll have missed Her.

Indeed, the *dhikr* is like a broom that with the aid of the Master sweeps everything but God from the heart of the sufi—to the extent that even the dust of one's very being is swept away. Then the sufi proclaims:

I thought of You so often
that I completely became You.
Little by little You drew near,
and slowly but slowly I passed away.

Thus, the sufi is in constant remembrance of God.

The Sufi's Prayer

People pray in order to draw God's compassion and grace upon themselves. In their prayers, they beg God to bestow His benevolence upon them and not His wrath. But the sufi is one who is in love with the Beloved. Whether the Beloved is clothed in the garb of benevolence or wrath makes no difference. How, then, can the sufi pray for anything, when all he or she sees is the Beloved and not the outer garment?

One who prays to God for something prays from a 'self'. Such beseeching becomes a manifestation of an individual consciousness before Absolute Being. However, the enraptured lover cannot at all be conscious of his or her own existence before the Absolute, as that would be infidelity to the Beloved. Bāyazīd has said:

> From the time of my initiation into love, I have been ashamed to ask anything from God but God himself. Even to my daily prayers, required by religion, I always added, "Oh God, you know what Bāyazīd wants!"

In the words of Rūmī:

> *I know a group of saints;*
> *their mouths are shut to prayer.*

Since the sufis want only what God wants, and have no 'self' from which to pray, how can they pray for anything? Indeed, how can 'they' pray at all?

Thus, when the sufi prays, 'he' or 'she' is not praying and consequently cannot pray for anything.

The Repentance of the Sufi

Ordinary people repent from their past misdeeds. Ascetics renounce the world as a whole. The sufis, however, give up both this world and the next. Ordinary people repent in the hope of a better future; ascetics repent for the promise of heaven. But the sufis, in God's Love, let go of everything.

In feeling repentant for their past misdeeds, people have themselves in mind. Since the sufi is nobody, no-self, there can be no repentance for him or her. In other words, as the expression of repentance is a sign of 'self'-existence and sufis in love have given up this 'self', they even 'repent from repentance' or 'let go of letting go'. Concerning this, the Prophet has said:

> *Your very being and existence*
> *is a sin which is like no other sin.*

It is reported that Ḥallāj once asked Ibrāhīm al-Khawwāṣ what spiritual station he had reached. Ibrāhīm replied, "I am in the station of complete trust in God (*tawakkul*)." Ḥallāj exclaimed in sorrow, "O lose yourself. Then there'll be no need to trust in God."

Thus, in and through God's Love, the sufi lets go of everything, even this letting go.

The Asceticism of the Sufi

Ascetics turn away from this world toward the hereafter. Sufis turn away from both this world and the next, inclining toward God alone. In turning away from the pleasures of this world, the ascetics want to gain the pleasures of heaven. The sufis, however, enraptured in Divine Love, pass from themselves and forget entirely about gain, loss or pleasure—here or hereafter. By thinking of and delighting in the future rewards of heaven, ascetics are, in fact, merely engaging in a subtle form of self-gratification and self-worship. Sufis though, drunk through Union with God, are totally absorbed in the present moment, the 'here and now', and have let go of existence.

As Bāyazīd has said, "The duration of Bāyazīd's life of asceticism was only three days. On the first day, he renounced the world. On the second day, he renounced the hereafter. And on the last day, he renounced whatever separated him from God."

Thus, the asceticism of the sufi is in renouncing and letting go of everything that is other than God.

The Inward Journey and the Outward Manner

Traveling on the path of the sufis involves both an inward journey and an outward manner.

The outward manner is a necessary part of the path because the inward journey alone cannot take one to perfection. On the voyage towards perfection, sufis must master outward manner as well as complete the inward journey, so that they live in harmony with all people at all times.

Sufis, in every way, move towards perfection. Inwardly, they do so through being taken up by the pull of God. Outwardly, they do so by living in harmony with all. This proper 'outward manner' is so necessary on the path that some sufis have considered it even more important than the inward journey. For example, when Rūmī was called upon to show his master (Shams-i Tabrīzī) the stage of his perfection, he refrained from speaking of his inner knowledge and spiritual insight. Instead, he declared:

O Master of lovers, have you ever seen
a more harmonious being than I,
Alive with the living and dead with the dead?

Thus, the sufi is inwardly burning with the fire of love, while outwardly living in harmony with everyone.

The Solitude of the Sufi

Although sufis live outwardly among people, inwardly they are constantly occupied with God. Their bodies and minds exist with others, whereas their hearts are far from them. Externally, they are congenial with everyone. Inwardly, however, they are strangers to all. They are at peace with all people, yet within themselves tranquillity is to be found only in Divine Love. Though they live among people, truly they are alone.

Have you ever heard of a being
who is absent and present at the same time?
Such is my state, for I'm among the crowd,
while my heart has gone beyond.

Thus, the sufi is outwardly among people, while inwardly one with God.

The Self-Mortification and Seclusion of the Sufi

Self-mortification and going into seclusion are generally not practiced on the sufi path. However, as a result of the nourishment of love and absorption in God, while in the state of 'Divine Rapture', sufis may become unaware of their physical needs, as well as of the people around them. The rapture of love may even draw them to such an extent that they become unaware of being lovers. Sufis in this state have no will of their own; therefore they may not eat, and they may become cut off from people.

In the journey towards the Truth, sufis may sometimes mistakenly feel that as a result of their own efforts they move quickly on the path. Believing in this, they may strive intensely with their own will, thus causing the balance between their hearts and souls to become upset. In order to help such sufis regain an inner harmony, the master (or shaikh) may seclude them from other people for a time to make certain that they rest their minds, hearts and bodies. When they regain their balance, they then return to society.

In this case, seclusion and ascetic practice are specific instructions given by the master (or shaikh) to particular individuals, based upon their needs at that time in order to regain a state of peace and serenity. For most sufis, however, such practices are not permitted. They generally have no role in Sufism.

Thus, the sufi is not one who engages in either self-mortification or self-imposed seclusion.

The Visions and Miracles of the Sufi

In Sufism, paying attention to visions and miraculous occurrences only makes one's being impure. In such an impure state, one is manifesting existence and thus is unable to truly perform *namāz* (daily prayers). *Namāz* is the affirmation of Divine Unity. How then can one who is attending to and thus affirming the multiplicity at the surface of the Ocean of Oneness become drowned in its depths? As Maghribī has said:

Don't speak to us of visions and miracles,
for we have long ago transcended such things.
We saw them all to be illusion and dreams,
and dauntlessly we passed beyond them.

Thus, the sufi has nothing to do with visions and miracles.

The Proper Manner of the Sufi

The proper manner of the sufis involves letting go and giving up completely all self-worship, self-esteem, and attention to the 'self'. Such a way of being must first be observed and practiced in the heart of the sufi, until gradually it manifests itself in outward behavior. To assume a humble manner in outward actions, without being truly selfless in the heart, is of no value whatsoever in Sufism. In Rūmī's words:

Among those of the heart,
outward manner exists within.

As the masters of the path see through the outward manifestations of one's being to the true inner state, they are not fooled by external appearances. For example, the story is told of a disciple who was once in the presence of his master. He was standing with total reverence and respect, like one who is praying to God. The master said, "You are standing superbly, but it would be better if 'you' were not to be at all." All too often, as in the above story, excessive humility and self-abasement in outward manner are only indications of self-indulgence and self-conceit in one's inner being.

Thus, the proper manner of the sufi consists of selflessness in one's inner being which then manifests itself in one's actions.

The State of the Sufi

When sufis become surrendered to God, they truly believe that it is God who is the giver of all states. Therefore, they know that whatever state descends upon them comes from God, and they are fully content with it.

One of the shaikhs of Shāh Ni'matullāh was once in Māhān, the residence (and eventual burial place) of the master. For a length of time, he refrained from visiting the master. When he finally arrived, Shāh Ni'matullāh asked him why he hadn't come to visit earlier. The shaikh replied, "I was in such a negative state that I was afraid my presence would disturb the other sufis." The master asked him to describe his state. He said, "I was depressed, dismayed and totally disgusted with everyone and everything." The master then replied, "The destructive attribute of God was manifesting in you, and like all states, that was a good state." In other words, the shaikh's state was that of a man dead to the world, who was being controlled by the Divine Will. So, as with every other state, his state was a gift of God.

Thus, the sufi is always in a spiritual state.

The Patience of the Sufi

The 'self' or ego is affected by and reacts to the environment outside itself. The reactions that occur are expressed as anger, annoyance, impatience, desire and so forth. Sufis, however, have nothing to do with the ego, and have no 'self' from which to react. Therefore, they are not subject to these changing emotions and have no basis upon which to become offended by anyone, nor can they offend.

Good human beings control themselves and try never to annoy their fellow humans or inflict pain upon them, although they might occasionally experience offense in their interactions with others. The sufis, however, have neither the worldly passion to annoy or bring pain upon their fellow human beings nor the basis (a 'self') from which to become offended. Because the sufis have no 'self', there is no pain for them to bear; thus, they are unaffected by all the seeming vices and virtues of people. One who feels offended has a 'self', and one who still has a 'self' is not a sufi. Rather, he or she is one who remains caught up in 'duality' and is unfaithful to God. True sufis, however, are ever-faithful lovers of God, fully in the Oneness of God. As Ḥāfiẓ has said:

We offer love to everyone,
and in love accept all blame,
for on our path to be offended
is faithlessness to God.

Thus, the sufi can never experience offense.

The Desire of the Sufi

The desire of the sufi is the desire of the Beloved. According to the saying of the Prophet that "Islam is surrender", the sufi becomes totally surrendered to God's Will. Therefore, one who has a desire or will of one's own is not a sufi. In other words, the sufi is nothing and the Beloved is everything. As the sufi is nothing, nothing can be desired. A darvish was once asked, "What do you desire?" The darvish answered, "I desire not to desire."

Thus, the sufi has no desire.

The Sufi's Relationship to Others

People disagree with one another and become estranged because they have differing desires and self-interests. Sufis, however, are not concerned with gain or achievements such as wealth, power and social status. Therefore, they cannot disagree with or become estranged from anyone.

Whoever is a stranger to wealth,
fame and power,
is a friend to all.

—Sa'dī

That is to say, one whose heart is a stranger to all but God is a friend to everyone, as God is all that he or she sees. However, people who are conscious of themselves become estranged from others, and the more they are concerned with themselves, the more alienated from all humanity they become. Sufis, on the other hand, are friends to all, being strangers to themselves.

Thus, the sufi is friendly with everyone.

The Pure Heart of the Sufi

Hate and spite have no place in a heart where the love of God dwells. That is to say, a heart that is filled with malice and negativity cannot possibly contain Divine Love. Thus, free of hate, the sufi's heart contains and emanates only love. The following story is told in this regard:

> One day, Mālik Ashtar was going to the bazaar when someone who mistook him for an enemy came up and cursed him. After Mālik had departed, people came up and asked the man if he knew whom he had just cursed. He replied, "Yes, of course, that was one of my enemies." The people exclaimed, "No, you are mistaken. That was the famous sufi, Mālik Ashtar." Realizing his mistake, the man ran after Mālik and found him in the mosque doing *namāz*. After Mālik had finished his prayers, he was heard to add, "O God, I hold no hate in my heart for this man. I beseech you not to make it hard for him, and ask you to forgive him for what he has done."

In a similar vein, the following story is told about 'Alī, the disciple and spiritual successor of Muḥammad:

> When Ibn Muljam struck 'Alī with the poisoned sword, he was immediately seized and brought before the Master, 'Alī, who was still alive. 'Alī said to his son, Imām Ḥasan, "Now that he is your captive, treat him justly but with kindness."

Thus, whoever retains a grudge or has hate in his or her heart is not a sufi.

The Sufi and Material Wealth

Some people believe that a sufi must be without wealth. Actually, this is an incorrect view. To willfully insist upon living in poverty is itself an attachment. The sufi, though, is free from all attachment. The essential point here is that the sufi's heart should have no attachment to wealth or worldly possessions. If a sufi is rich one day, then poor the next, he or she remains unaffected by either condition.

The story is told of a darvish who went to visit an honorable and wealthy shaikh. Seeing the shaikh's affluence, the darvish thought, "How can Sufism and such prosperity go hand-in-hand?" After staying a few days with the shaikh, the darvish decided to leave. The shaikh said, "Let me accompany you on your journey."

After they had gone a short distance, the darvish suddenly noticed that he had forgotten his *kashkūl*.[1] So he asked the shaikh for permission to return and get it. The shaikh replied, "I departed from all my possessions, but you can't leave behind even your begging bowl. Therefore, we must part company here."

Thus, the sufi is not attached to either wealth or poverty.

The Sufi in the 'Tavern of Ruin'

In the state of 'passing away of the self in God' (*fanā'*), the sufi has completely lost the 'self' and reached the spiritual station that is called the 'Tavern of Ruin'. It is said that Bāyazīd was in this station when someone knocked at his door. Bāyazīd asked, "Who do you want?" The man answered that he was looking for Bāyazīd. Bāyazīd replied, "Ah! It has been years since I have had any news of him."

In such a state, the sufi has passed beyond faith and unbelief, seeing neither friend nor stranger; in every place and in everyone, he or she sees only God. Yet, it is not from the self that he or she sees. Rather, it is God seeing God in God. In such a state, the sufi says:

The lover has died and left behind
both Islam and unbelief.
Burning in love of the flame,
the moth does not distinguish
between the light of the mosque
and the light of the monastery.

Or:

Blasphemy and religion, Ka'ba and
pagan temple,
for the true lover, are one and the same.

Thus, the sufi in the 'Tavern of Ruin', having died to and passed away from self, is liberated from both blasphemy and religion.

The Dance of the Sufi

The enrapturing of the sufis by God, or rather the 'pull' of God, keeps the sufi continually in spiritual inner dance and movement. Whenever a wave of such Divine rapture strikes the heart of the sufi, it creates turbulence in his or her inner being. This, in turn, causes the body to move. Upon seeing such movement, non-sufis have often supposed that the sufi is dancing. In reality, however, it is the waves of the Ocean of the Truth that are tossing and turning the anchorless vessel that is the heart of the sufi.

Some superficial people have supposed that by dancing one can become Divinely enraptured and reach God. While it is true that all dancing can undoubtedly give one a feeling of intoxication, this kind of dancing is willful. However, sufis in love have no will of their own, and therefore dance involuntarily. Their feet dance upon both worlds, and their hands let go of all the beauty of paradise. They have given up all thought of existence.

Thus, the sufi comes to 'dance' only when taken from himself or herself.

The Death of the Sufi

The sufi considers death to be a degree of perfection. It is by means of death that one comes closer to God. Since the sufi knows that true life is only in death, he or she arrives (before the death of the physical body) at the death of the 'self', through both the pull of love and the step of inner struggle. With each breath, a quality of the 'self' dies, and an attribute of God is born, until eventually the 'self' dies away altogether. In this way, the sufi comes alive through God and in God. This is the inner meaning of the Prophet's saying, "Die before you die," as well as of the following verse by Rūmī:

Lovers die a different death
at every moment,

and the kinds of death they die
are not just one.

Thus, the sufi dies at every moment.

The Paradise of the Sufi

The sufi dwells in the paradise of being One with the Beloved in the here and now, not looking to the promised paradise of the hereafter:

As I am in paradise now,
why should I care about the ascetic's promise
of paradise tomorrow?

For the sufi, one who does not find the Truth in this world will not reach it in the next. As it is written in the Koran, "Whoever is blind in this world will be blind in the next, and go yet further astray" (17:72).

Whoever does not see the face
of the Beloved today
is not likely to see it tomorrow.

Thus, the sufi is in paradise in this world.

The Sufi's Happiness

For most people, happiness results from the attainment of desire or the avoidance of unpleasantness. For the sufi, however, true happiness comes from giving up the 'self'. As long as you are 'you', you will be miserable and impoverished. But when your 'self' has passed away, you are the Beloved—contented and fulfilled. The sufi knows that all the disturbances, anxieties, discontent and emptiness of humanity arise from the dichotomy of 'I' and 'you' (that is, from having a 'self'). For this reason, the sufi lets the 'self' die, and lives in inner peace.

Thus, for the sufi, the only true happiness is in giving up the 'self'.

The Sufi's View of Time

Sufis do not think about the past or future. They are completely absorbed in the present, the 'here and now'. In this regard, the sufis have a saying, "Breath is a Godsend." Some superficial people may use such an idea to justify being lax, irresponsible and lazy. But the sufi's dependence on the present moment makes him or her fully grasp the significance of every breath, every moment. Consequently, not even for a moment do sufis forget their Divine aim. At each moment, they are in remembrance of God, purifying themselves and serving people, never postponing until tomorrow what must be done today. This is the profound meaning of the expression "Breath is a Godsend." As Rūmī has said:

O friend, the sufi is the child
of the moment.
On the path, talk of tomorrow
has no place.

Or in the words of Shāh Ni'matullāh:

Abandon these tales of yesterday
and tomorrow.
Now is the time to change yourself!

When the sufi passes beyond time and space, he or she travels from pre-eternity to post-eternity in one breath. In such a state, the period from pre-eternity to post-eternity is, indeed, only one breath. If then asked about pre-eternity, the sufi, like Junayd, would reply, "Pre-eternity is now," meaning, "For me there is no creation; in my eyes there is only the Creator."

Thus, the sufi never loses sight of the unique importance of this very moment and every breath.

The Sufi's Separation and Union

The sufi is intensely in love with God, whether God seems near or far away. Hope of being united with the Beloved, or fear of being apart, involves the banality of thinking that God will either reward one with union for one's efforts or punish one with separation for one's failings. Moreover, this attitude reduces one's relationship with God to the level of trading or bargaining. The sufi, however, neither hopes for union nor fears separation. Rather, as a true lover, he or she expects nothing of the Beloved.

Some perfect sufis have even esteemed separation higher than union. In this view, union is but an aspiration of the lover, whereas separation is what the Beloved desires. For such sufis, a lover, in the truest sense, desires only what the Beloved desires.

Another group of sufi shaikhs has considered the agony of union to be more intense than the pain of separation. In the words of Jāmī:

In union, there is the fear
of annihilation.
Whereas in separation, there is
the hope of union.

Thus, in the end, the sufi is concerned with neither union nor separation, but only with the Beloved.

The Sufi's View of Divine Benevolence and Divine Wrath

Sufis see benevolence and wrath—both qualities of God—as two sides of the same coin. As they are the lovers of the 'coin' itself, it matters not which side shows its face. They are in love with both countenances of the Beloved.

I love both the Beloved's
benevolence and wrath.
How strange that I should
adore these opposites.

—Rūmī

The one who delights in the Beloved's benevolence but not in the Beloved's wrath is not a sufi. As Ḥāfiẓ has said:

On this path, whatever happens,
whether benevolence or wrath,
is always for the best.

Thus, the sufi is equally in love with both faces of the Beloved.

The Unity of the Sufi

Sufis are those whose hearts are filled with the love of God and who pay attention to nothing else. Although there may be many sufis, truly all are one. In their spiritual lives, all have a single goal and purpose. Their hearts are all directed towards the One, and they seek nothing but the Essence of God. In the words of Rūmī:

The souls of wolves and dogs
are separate from one another.

But the souls of those of God
are all united.

Or, as it is stated in the Sayings of the Prophet: "The believers are all as one soul." Rūmī further illustrates the point with this story:

> In a court of justice requiring several witnesses to prove guilt, a prosecutor brought a few sufis to bear witness with regard to a certain crime. The judge, however, refused to accept the testimony on the grounds that the prosecutor had only one witness, a thousand sufis being the same as one.

Thus, all sufis, though physically separate, are one.

The World of the Sufi

There is no aggressiveness or spite in the world of the sufis. Everywhere, peace prevails and conflict has no place; hypocrisy and deceit do not exist. Each sufi seeks earnestly to serve his or her fellow sufis. Here, one can find only purity, tranquillity and love. Truly, this is the utopia that all hearts desire; it is paradise realized in this very world.

In the realm of the sufis, all love one another—regardless of the superficial distinctions of race, wealth and social status. Under the banner of humanity, all help one another. The conflicts that so often stem from being caught up in the realm of 'I' and 'you' do not exist for the sufi. Rather, each sufi is a mirror for the other sufis and all reflect the Truth.

Thus, the world of the sufi is the world that all truly desire in their hearts.

1 *kashkūl*: a begging bowl or container that in the past was carried by wandering darvishes and that is presently used as a symbol of spiritual poverty in the emblem of the Nimatullahi Sufi Order.

Love

Sufism is a way to God through love.

In Persian, the term used by the sufis for love is *'ishq*, a word derived from *'ashaqah*, which is a type of vine. When this vine winds itself around a tree, the tree withers and dies. So, too, love of the world dries up and turns yellow the tree of the body. But spiritual love withers the root of the self.

Love from the Viewpoint of Islam

In the Koran, God proclaims, "Those who believe have great love for God" (2:165). This intensity of love is called *'ishq*. The Prophet Muḥammad has declared, "Those who have intense love for God are virtuous in love, and keep their lovemaking hidden from others; when they die, they will undoubtedly die as martyrs." In a prophetic tradition (*ḥadīth*), God says to Muḥammad:

Whoever seeks Me will find Me.
Whoever I love, I will kill, and
Whoever I kill, his blood money will I pay:
I Myself am his blood money.

In a prayer, Muḥammad said, "I pray to see Thy Face and I long for Thy sight." Imām Ḥusayn has said:

> Thou art the One who removes 'that which is other' from the hearts of those who love Thee, until in their hearts there is only Thy love.

Knowledge and Love

The end result of *maḥabba* (loving-kindness) is *'ishq* (love). *'Ishq* is the supreme and most fervent kind of love. *'Ishq* is more special and pure than *maḥabba*, since *'ishq* is a result of *maḥabba*, but not all *maḥabba* leads to *'ishq*. *Maḥabba*, however, is on a higher level than gnosis (*ma'rifa*), since *maḥabba* arises from gnosis, but not all gnosis leads to *maḥabba*.

Instinctive Love, Spiritual Love and Divine Love

In instinctive love, lovers long for the beloved for their own sake. In spiritual love, lovers long for the beloved for their own sake, as well as for that of the beloved. In Divine Love, however, lovers long for the Beloved not for themselves, but only for the sake of the Beloved. As Rūmī has said in the *Mathnawī*:

> *For those who love Him, He alone*
> *is their joy and sorrow.*
> *He alone is their recompense and reward.*
> *If anything other than the Beloved is seen,*
> *then it is not love, but mere passion.*
> *Love is that flame which when it blazes up*
> *consumes all but the Beloved Himself.*

Real Love and Temporal Love

Temporal love arises from the beauty of transient forms. Like them, it is also transient—its only lasting result being the perpetuation of the species. It is the product of the sublimation and refinement of sexual desire. Real or Divine Love, however, is a profusion and rapture from the Absolute Beloved which descends upon the heart of the sincere lover. This lover is like a moth fluttering around the beauty of the candle that is the Absolute, burning away its relative existence in God's fire. The lover turns away from the self and perishes, inclines towards God and becomes alive. When the lover is emptied of self and becomes nothing, he or she finds eternal life.

A few sufi masters have considered Real Love to grow out of temporal love, and indeed it is possible for temporal love to create a vessel for receiving the outpouring of Real Love. In the words of Rūmī, "His aim was the form, but through it, he finally found God." Regarding the difference between Real and temporal love, Rūmī has said:

Hey! Drink this fine fiery wine, these needles of fire,
And fall so drunk that you will not wake on the Day of
Resurrection.
In this godly wine, you will find youthful spirit.
In the fire of instinct, you will never find such unerring fidelity.

Love in Sufism

Generally speaking, human beings' love is the result of God's Love, love being one of God's attributes. But more precisely, love is an attribute of the Divine Will, Will being an attribute of the Divine Essence.

When love (*'ishq*) acts on anything that exists, it is called 'will', and the creation of living beings is one of its results. When love embraces the elect, or those whom God has chosen, it is called 'mercy', and when love embraces the elect of the elect it is called 'bounty'. This bounty is given only to humanity, and it completes the bounties of the Benefactor. As is said in the Koran, "I completed My bounty unto you" (5:3). This verse refers to that same bounty and favor that is called 'sainthood' (*walāyah*).

By virtue of this favor, by the attracting force of "He loves them," God burns away the lover's existence as lover and brings him or her to the state of *fanā'* ('passing away of the self in God'). Then, by the illumination that manifests the Divine Attributes of the Beloved, the lover is drawn from the state of *fanā'* to the state of *baqā'* ('permanence in the Beloved'). In this state, the relative existence of the lover has gone and Absolute Existence has become manifest. Here, by the light of God, Reality can be perceived as it truly is. This is the meaning of the Prophet's saying, "O God, show me all things as they really are." Rūzbihān has said:

Love is a sword that cuts away the lover's temporal

> existence. Love is that perfection which comes from the perfection of the Absolute. When It unites with the lover, the lover will cease to be a mere slave and will no longer be caught up in the temporal world. Outwardly, such a one will reveal the Divine Majesty; inwardly, that one will attain the level of Lordship. It cannot be said that the lover dies, for death does not hold sway over one who lives by God's love.

Sufis believe that the foundation of the created world is love. All motion, activity and light throughout the entire universe as we know it derive from the rays of love, and true perfection must be sought in and through love. Some sufis have said, "Love is the totality of all the perfections that are in the essence of an individual, and this entirety can only be an attribute of the Absolute." For the same reason, 'Irāqī considered love to be the Essence of Absolute Oneness. Mīr Ḥusaynī Harawī has said:

> *Love* ('ishq) *is a shining star in the heaven of Reality.*
> *It is one step above* maḥabba.
> *Faith and unbelief are one and the same to love.*
> *It craves neither doubt nor certainty.*
> *It is a diver in the Absolute's Ocean, its ship the spirit.*
> *Indeed, love is the dissolver of all difficulties,*
> *And the polisher of the mirror of the heart.*

Heart and Love

The soul encompasses the body; the heart encompasses both the soul and the body; and love is the ruler of the heart. Some sufis have said, "The house of the heart must be emptied of everything other than love so that love can reside there." However, this is an intellectual explanation. For love, when it comes, burns and annihilates everything but the Beloved. Thus, by itself, love empties the house.

Intellect and Love

In discussing the intellect and love from the point of view of Sufism, what is usually meant by the intellect is reason or the particular intellect. But, in fact, the perfection of Divine Love manifests itself as the Universal Intellect; the perfection of love is the same as the Universal Intellect.

Reason says, "There can be no more
than four dimensions; more are impossible."
Love answers, "The way beyond exists and I
have been there many times."

Rūmī has said:

What then is love? The ocean of nonexistence;
There, the foot of the intellect is dissolved.

Intellect is always busy doing things, while love rests, free of all these imaginary activities. Intellect has knowledge and eloquence, while love is free from both worlds.

Intellect says, "I know the subtleties of wonderful things." Love says, "Without the Beloved, all your words are just empty breath." Mīr Ḥusaynī Harawī has written:

Intellect says, "I do useful things."
Love says, "I risk all."
Intellect builds, saying, "This is fine here."
Love burns, saying, "This is contaminated here."
Intellect laughs, saying, "This is only name and fame."
Love flies away, saying, "This is only bait and trap."

Shaikh Najm al-Dīn Rāzī, in his book, *Intellect and Love*, compares intellect to water and love to fire.

> Intellect travels in the world of being and has the attributes of water. Everywhere it goes, it flows like water and the two worlds flourish. But love has the attributes of fire and travels in the World of Non-being. Everywhere it goes, it burns; everything it touches is annihilated.

In our view, under certain conditions, the particular intellect or reason and the love of this world can be like both water and fire. When the mind makes use of positive feelings, what results is an intellect that has the attributes of water. It brings about prosperity. Its investigations and innovations serve humanity.

On the other hand, when the mind acts without regard for positive feelings and rushes into the battlefield of life, what results is a reason that has the attributes of fire, destroying mankind and causing conflict and war.

If, however, these positive feelings harness the mind, what results is a love that has the attributes of water. Wherever it flows, others flourish and the self is emptied. This love serves others selflessly, as a cloud pours life-giving rain onto the field of all creation.

If these positive feelings do not consider the mind or are not able to make use of the mind, and go tearing wildly across the battlefield alone (with only selfish desires), the result is a love that has the attributes of fire. On behalf of the self, such a love burns up everything. In order to achieve its selfish desires, it actually destroys others.

Thus, according to the different states and interactions of the mind and positive feelings, various kinds of love and reason become manifested. In the highest state, when Divine Love obtains the services of the perfect mind, true love appears. The fullness that is experienced then is described in the Koran as, "I have completed my bounty unto you" (5:3).

Love in the West and Love in Sufism

In the minds of Westerners, love is usually understood as the attraction or positive feelings one has for other human beings, which at its higher levels helps an individual to be drawn to Reality. From this point of view, the lover must learn the ways of love. But this is very elementary.

For the sufis, love is not in the realm of sentiments or feelings. Rather, it is a Divine attraction, the drawing of the lover by God towards God. Here, the stress is not so much on the effort of the lover but rather on the pull of God. For this reason, Sufism says that love is "that which comes," like a raging flood, and the sufis look forward to its coming and carrying them away. As Rūmī has said:

The lovers (of God) have fallen into a fierce torrent.
They have surrendered themselves to the Beloved's Will.

Conclusion

Although words convey the perceptions of the soul, the soul is encompassed by the heart. And love is the ruler of the heart. Therefore, whatever can be said about love cannot truly express its essence, since love is beyond the realm of idle talk.

When I am in love, I am ashamed of all
I have ever said about love.

Although a commentary in words makes things clear,
wordless love is yet clearer and more illuminating...
Like the pen that was busily writing
until it came to love, and then split apart.

—Rūmī

Samā'

Our ecstasy in samā' *is no superficial experience,*
nor is this dance of ours something we do
for amusement.
Tell those who know nothing about it,
"O you without wisdom,
there would not be so much talk about samā'
if there were nothing essential in it."

—'Alā' al-Dawla Simnānī

Though usually translated as 'spiritual music', *samā'* literally means 'hearing'. In the terminology of Sufism, it is listening with the ear of the heart to music in the most profound sense—poetry, melodies, tunes and rhythmic harmonies—while being in a special state so deeply plunged in love that there is no taint of self left within awareness. In this sense, *samā'* is named the 'call of God'. Its reality is the wakefulness of the heart; its orientation is towards the Absolute. Sufis in the state of *samā'* are not paying attention to either this world or the next. The fire of love burns so intensely in them that everything but God is consumed. *Samā'* feeds that fire and gradually brings the Source of the sound and the listener closer and closer together until they become one.

The angelic or suprasensible world (*malakūt*) is the realm of true beauty. Whatever is fair, beautiful, or elegant (more precisely, whatever is harmonious) is a manifestation of the *malakūt*. *Samā'* puts us in contact with that world. By listening to mystical poetry and harmonious melodies, the heart of the sufi is directed towards that realm. As the Prophet has said, "God is beautiful and loves beauty." So *samā'*, with the aid of the light of God, shatters the dark mountain of worldly existence for those who sincerely love the Truth, making the path easy for them.

One of the sufi saints of Shiraz, Rūzbihān, once wrote, *"Samā'* is God's hearing; it is hearing from Him, for Him, in Him, and with Him. If it is not all of these at the same time, the person practicing *samā'* is not being faithful to God."

In the *samā'* of the sufis, anyone who remains aware of self and is not wholly taken up with God is not worthy of *samā'*. Therefore, it is only suitable for the perfect. Rūzbihān has also said:

Shorn of the worldly desires and passions of the self,
disciples of love hear samā'.
Cut off from their own minds,
seekers yearning for God hear samā'.
Deprived of their hearts,
those enamored of love hear samā'.
Those who have gone beyond even their spirit,
who are totally lost in nearness to God, hear samā'.
If, on the contrary, hearing is with the worldly self,
mind, heart, or spirit,
Then one is still veiled from God.

When sufis become selfless, when lovers become sincere, they hear the call of God in every sound. In every melody, the Beloved beckons. No longer does the cell of seclusion or the assembly of the sufis, being alone or being in a crowd, have any meaning. In every place, in every state, sufis see only the manifestation of Divine Beauty and hear only the harmonious sounds of the Beloved. Sometimes they ride the surging waves of *samā'*, drunk but still existing; other times they abandon existence altogether in the Ocean of Oneness. Sometimes like 'Alī, the first master of the sufis, they will hear church bells singing, "God is pure, God is my Lord, everlasting and in need of nothing." Like Shiblī (a sufi saint of the ninth century A.D.), they may hear the sound of *'hū, hū'* (God's name) in the cooing of the ringdove. Like Maghribī (a famous sufi of the fourteenth century A.D.), they may hear 'Allāh,

Allāh' in the ordinary sound of the turning of a water-wheel. Such is the *samā‘* of perfect beings and pure-hearted lovers of God. Another sufi, Mīr Ḥusaynī Harawī, has said:

Those masters of mystical states have well proclaimed
that if you are still you, this wine is forbidden.
Where a hundred thousand great lovers become lost,
it is better that the beginner stay far away.
If you have not given up pursuing worldly passions and desires,
how could samā‘ *ever be permitted for you?*
This delight is not for every thirsty tippler;
only a heart full of light is worthy of it.
It is the way of those who sacrifice all for God,
not the haven of a handful of impudent hypocrites.

With the passing of time, some of the seekers on the sufi path found delight in the *samā‘* of the perfect sufis and turned towards it in order to receive help from it. There is a saying of the Prophet, "Whoever imitates a people is one of them." Some, however, who did not know the secrets of *samā‘* imitated this second group, simply for self-gratification and to enliven their gatherings and retreats. In this way, the *'samā‘* of self-seeking' and the *'samā‘* of reason' emerged and became distinguished from the *'samā‘* of love.' In the *Mathnawī*, Rūmī has said:

Not everyone is a master of the real samā‘;
not every bird is able to eat figs,
Certainly not a dead bird, rotting,
full of illusions, ignorant and blind.

When those dominated by their reason turned to *samā‘*, they enumerated various kinds of *samā‘*, which they considered lawful or unlawful in order to justify their *samā‘* and differentiate it from the *samā‘* of those dominated by their worldly selves. They also established rules of decorum for listening to *samā‘* and found, or else manufactured, various traditional sayings to support their views. For example, 'Ā'isha, the wife of the Prophet, told the following story:

> Once there was a woman in my house who was singing when 'Umar (the second Caliph) asked permission to enter. The woman, upon recognizing 'Umar 's voice, hid herself. When 'Umar entered the house, the Prophet, who had been

> listening to this singing, was smiling. 'Umar said, "O Prophet of God, why are you smiling?" He replied, "There was a woman here who was singing, but when she heard your voice she hid herself." Then 'Umar said, "I will not leave this house unless I hear what the Prophet has heard." So the Prophet called the woman and she resumed her singing while the Prophet and 'Umar listened.

There is another tale recounted by a companion of the Prophet, Mālik ibn Anas:

> I was with the Prophet when the Archangel Gabriel descended and announced, "O Prophet of God, the poor among your people will enter Paradise five hundred years sooner than the rich." Upon hearing this, the Prophet became happy and asked, "Is there anyone among you who can sing?" A Bedouin replied, "Yes, O Prophet of God." The Prophet said, "Come forward." The Bedouin did so and began to sing: "Love, like a venomous snake, has tormented my heart, but for this illness there is neither physician nor sorcerer. Only my Beloved, with whom I am so much in love, can cure me, for He possesses the medicines and incantations for my malady."
>
> When the Prophet heard this song, he went into a state of rapture and his companions became full of joy. From the intensity of that state, the Prophet's cloak fell from his shoulders. When their bliss passed, they all went back to their own places. Then 'Mu'āwiya, one of the Prophet's companions, said, "O Prophet, that was enjoyable." The Prophet replied, 'Mu'āwiya! What are you saying? He who does not become totally transported upon hearing the Beloved's name in *samā'* is not a noble man, worthy of honor." Then the Prophet tore his cloak into four hundred pieces and gave them to the crowd of those present.

This tradition is usually attributed to the Prophet in order to show that listening to music, going into a state of ecstasy, tearing one's clothes and distributing the pieces among the people present are customs sanctioned by the Prophet himself. (All of these things eventually became customary among certain of the later sufi shaikhs). It is a tradition that became a pretext in the hands of intellectuals who wanted to show that in the way of love reason also has a role to play.

Classifications of *Samā'* and Its Practitioners

Rūzbihān has categorized three types of *samā'*:

> There is one type of *samā‘* for the common people, one for the elect, and one for the elect among the elect. The common people listen through their worldly natures and inclinations, and that is destitution. The elect listen with the heart and that is seeking. The elect among the elect listen with the soul and that is being in love. If I express myself in these words, it is only to prevent those who have not arrived from becoming enmeshed in false conjectures, and to prevent those who are not on the path from wasting their time.

A saint of the tenth century A.D., Abū ‘Alī Daqqāq, once said:

> There are three groups who practice *samā‘*. The first attempt or pretend to practice; the second hear but only passively; the third are able to listen actively. The first hear at the times specified for *samā‘*. The second group hear by means of the heart. But only those who really listen, listen by, with, and to God.

Another sufi shaikh, Abū Bakr of Mecca, has written:

> The *samā‘* of the common people arises from following their own worldly natures and inclinations. The *samā‘* of the disciples on the path arises from their desire for Truth, and not following the worldly tendencies of the self. The *samā‘* of the saints comes from perceiving the bounties and riches of God. The *samā‘* of the gnostics is through mystical contemplation, as God witnessing God. And the *samā‘* of those at one with the Absolute comes from God's direct unveiling. For each of these groups, there is a degree and a station.

So, too, Abū ‘Uthmān Ḥīrī, a sufi of the ninth century A.D., has written:

> There are three types of *samā‘*: the *samā‘* of the beginners, the *samā‘* of the sincere, and the *samā‘* of the gnostics. The beginners desire a high spiritual station and as a result fall into temptation and hypocrisy. The sincere seek from *samā‘* a greater intensity in their spiritual states, and each hears that which corresponds to his or her state at that moment. The gnostics are those who persevere on the path; in *samā‘*, their consciousness is with God rather than with whatever comes into their hearts or minds from either movement or stillness.

It is also said that those who practice *samā‘* can be divided into the following three groups: those of the Divine truths (i.e., the prophets), those who supplicate, and those of the contented poor (i.e., the sufis). The *samā‘*

of those of the Divine truths reaches a state in which they are addressed by God. Those who supplicate address God in their hearts in the form of meanings that they hear. They are truthful in what they say to God. The contented poor (the true sufis) have cut themselves off from attachments to the world with all its adversities; they hear *samā'* with pure hearts. They are the ones nearest to God.

Instances of Lawful and Unlawful *Samā'*

When God's *samā'* became mixed with the *samā'* of His creatures, and instead of being reserved for the elect of the elect became accessible to the elect, and to the common people as well, then true *samā'* left the hands of love and fell into the grip of reason, which seeks what is expedient for peoples' welfare. Then, reason, fearing the seductions of the worldly self, distinguished the lawfulness or unlawfulness of *samā'* in different circumstances. It had no alternative but to do so.

Abū 'Alī Daqqāq put this well when he explained, "*Samā'* is unlawful for the common people because of the persistence of their worldly selves. It is permissible for those who are able to abstain from the desires of their worldly selves because of their efforts in the way of God, and it is recommended for our companions because their hearts are alive."

Ghazālī has categorized *samā'* in this way:

1. Unlawful *samā'*: *Samā'* is unlawful for adolescents and those in whom worldly passion is still uppermost, as it would stimulate these reprehensible qualities which could dominate them.

2. *Samā'* is to be discouraged for those in whom it might become a habit and who would always participate in it as if it were merely an amusement.

3. *Samā'* is permissible for those who can listen to its pleasing sound purely for enjoyment.

4. *Samā'* is recommended for those in whom it increases the love of God, and who are moved by it towards only praiseworthy qualities.

Why did Ghazālī not mention obligatory *samā'*? One may suppose that he considered obligatory *samā'* to be beyond the range of reason and mere words, and that he therefore reserved it for the true lovers, the elect of the elect.

The Rules of Conduct During *Samā'*

In *samā'* sessions of the sufis, the following rules must be observed:

1. Until the state of *samā'* spontaneously arises in one, it is not permitted.

2. One must not make a habit of *samā'*, since like any other habit, it would be blameworthy.

3. *Samā'* must not be done too often or it will no longer evoke special veneration.

4. There must be no *samā'* without a sufi master or shaikh (or authorized person) being present.

5. The general public, or those not on the path, should not be present.

6. One must act with respect toward the singer and the musicians.

7. Those participating in *samā'* must not approach it as if it were merely an amusing pastime.

8. One must not pretend to be in the state of *samā'*.

9. If the state of *samā'* does not arise, one must not try to force it to come, but if the state happens, one should not resist it. In other words, if God moves you, allow yourself to be moved; if God does not, simply be still.

10. If the power of worldly instinct arises, it should be seen for what it is and not confused with the genuine spiritual ecstasy of *samā'*.

11. In the state of *samā'*, one should not seek help from others. If, however, assistance is offered, it should not be rejected.

12. Without the permission of the shaikh, one must not interfere in the *samā'* of others.

13. During the *samā'* session, one must not lean on or against anything; this is symbolic of the fact that one must rely only on God.

14. In the *samā'* session, one must not imitate anybody.

15. Without the permission of the shaikh, a beginner should not attend a *samā'* session.

16. One who seeks to participate in *samā'* must have a heart free from worldly passion, one filled with the purity of the light of the worship of God. Furthermore, one's heart must be sincerely and wholly receptive and present in the presence of God. Then, while in *samā'*, such a person will be far away from the temptations of the worldly self.

17. The *samā'* of those who are strangers to spiritual states, and who in their hearts have no relation with God, is tainted with self and, therefore, imperfect. Those who engage in *samā'* while in this state (assuming they are aware of it) have deviated from the true path. If they are ignorant of these limitations, and consider *samā'* as stemming from themselves rather than from God, then they have become dualists. Such people have in effect denied God. They consider Satan's whisperings to be Divine inspiration, and the desire of their worldly selves to be God's will. It is in reference to this that it has been said, "*Samā'* can only be advised for one whose worldly self is dead and whose heart is alive."

18. During *samā'* one must sit properly (see p. 168).

19. At the time of *samā'* one must sit with head lowered, absorbed in the remembrance of God in one's heart, not looking at others, just as one sits for daily prayers. In this way, the hearts of all participants will be one with God.

20. The singer and musicians of the *samā'* session must be sufis who feel the pain of separation from God. They must not come to the gathering for the purpose of making money or earning a living.

It has been said that in the days of Junayd, *samā'* was very popular. This was a time when many shaikhs and groups of sufis were beginning to appear. One day towards the end of a *samā'* session, it was noticed that Junayd was not singing. His disciples asked him, "Why are you not singing?" He said, "With whom can I do so?" They said, "With yourself." Then he asked, "From whom shall I listen?" They replied, "From yourself."

This story indicates that *samā'* should be practiced with a group of those who have similar aspirations, so that all can listen together with the same pain of separation and sing with the same sincerity and devotion. Even at that time, however, those who both felt such pain and could sing with sincerity and devotion were rarely to be found.

Why Sufis Do Not Recite the Koran During *Samā‘* but Instead Use *Dhikr* and Poetry

Ghazālī has said, "There have been many times when sufis listening to the Koran being sung experienced great ecstasy. Many people in such sessions became unconscious; some even died." Therefore, instead of singing verses of the Koran, sufis have usually used poetry and *dhikr*s to help them keep the remembrance of God constant in their hearts. Other reasons for this are:

1. All verses of the Koran are not suitable for the various states of the lovers of God.

2. Most Muslims know the Koran and read it often; normally when anything is heard repeatedly it will no longer be able to move the heart.

3. Most hearts can be moved only when they are stimulated by rhythmic vibrations, harmonies and melodies. The state of *samā‘* seldom occurs while people are listening to prose. Since it would be inappropriate to set the Koran to music, the sufis listen instead to harmonious songs.

Situations in Which *Samā‘* Is Not Allowed

In arranging a *samā‘* session, one must consider the time, the place, and the people taking part.

Samā‘ is prohibited at times when one's heart is paying attention to anything other than God, when it is time for prayer, or when the heart and mind are scattered (as, for example, when one is hungry or one's stomach is full).

As regards the place, *samā‘* is not permitted where the environment is disturbing or unpleasant, such as in the houses of unjust people. The reason for this is that such places upset the mind. As for the people participating, one should not engage in *samā‘* under the following conditions:

1. There is someone present who is proud and caught up in worldly affairs.

2. The singer does not believe in what the sufis believe.

3. One of those present continually pretends to be dancing or moving as if selflessly, or tries to put himself or herself into a state of ecstasy.

4. There is a group present who neglects the remembrance of God and takes part in *samāʿ* from erroneous thought, instead of from God.

5. Those present discuss ordinary things, let their attention wander, or lack respect for the *samāʿ* session.

6. Young people are present who are strongly dominated by their worldly selves.

7. Those attending are not free from thoughts of one another. It is related that Mushtāq, a sufi shaikh of the eighteenth century A.D., in one of his *samāʿ* sessions suddenly raised his head and said to his disciples, "There is something present which is interfering with our *samāʿ*. If there is anyone among you who has a dispute with another, he must leave the gathering." At this point, two brothers who had been quarreling about some inherited land came forward and were reconciled with one another.

8. Either ascetics or worldly people are present, since the ascetic is likely to have a critical attitude toward *samāʿ*, and the person whose attention remains on worldly matters may pretend to be in ecstasy when he or she is not.

The Benefits of *Samāʿ*

Samāʿ is like the sun: it caresses and inflames, melts and burns.

1. Sometimes the beginners on the path find that their hearts become weary. As a result of this weariness, their states may become languid and they may neglect their spiritual practices. To correct this, some sufi masters have prescribed listening to spiritual music, pure sounds that lead one back toward God, appropriate melodies and spiritually uplifting poetry. All this, of course, must come within the bounds permitted by the religion.

2. As a result of the tendencies of the worldly self, beginners may find there are ‘veils’ that prevent them from realizing higher states of consciousness. If this leads to a rather prolonged separation from such higher states (as may well occur), the fire of love's longing can greatly diminish. When this happens, a love song describing the state of separation may enable beginners to recover their motivation and renew their wish for the Truth, as a result of which the veil will be lifted.

3. It can happen during *samā‘* that the whole spiritual path can be traversed in a few moments of rapture, of being intensely drawn by the Beloved. In this state, the seeker can even shake off the dust of being, the taint of his or her compulsive conditioning in time, and realize the timeless Oneness of God.

Differences Among Sufis in the Practice of *Samā‘* and in its Effects

1. Some shaikhs have become so drowned in the Ocean of God that the world around them, with all its sounds and melodies, has no effect on them. It is said that Mamshād Dināwarī, a well-known Sufi at the time, was passing by a group of beginners who were practicing *samā‘*. When they saw him, they stopped. He said, “Continue with what you were doing. Even if all the distractions of the world were gathered together in my ears, they would not be able to divert me from my aim, nor would they cure my pain.”

2. A few sufi masters have been continuously in a state of witnessing God. Here again, *samā‘* has no effect on them. It is said that Sahl ibn ‘Abdullāh, a sufi shaikh of the ninth century A.D., declared, “My state before praying is the same as my state in prayer.” This indicates that he had reached the state of witnessing God all the time. The state of one who has attained such a spiritual station is the same during *samā‘* as it was before it.

3. Sufi masters have considered *samā‘* to be a generator of difficulty for some, a help for others, and a means of increasing direct knowledge of God for still others. Rūzbihān has said:

> *Samā‘* is only possible for those in a state of gnosis, experiencing direct knowledge of God. Since spiritual qualities are mixed with the body's worldly inclinations, until one has become free of these corrupting influences, one will not be receptive while in intimacy with God.

True *samā'* makes the mind tranquil and frees it from the heaviness of the ordinary human condition. It stimulates spiritual learning and discloses the secrets of God. For the imperfect, *samā'* will be a stumbling block or temptation, but for the perfect it will teach and guide. *Samā'* is not suitable for those who are merely living a life of worldly desires, who are dead in their hearts. For such people, it can only be harmful. However, *samā'* is obligatory for those whose hearts are alive, since in that state it is possible to travel the equivalent of a thousand years of the road of gnosis with one taste of *samā'*, a journey that cannot be accomplished by prayer or through performing any rite or ritual. As Rūmī has said:

> *Samā'* is the tranquillity of the soul of those who are alive. One knows *samā'* whose soul has a Soul (the Beloved). One who wants to be awakened by means of *samā'* is one who has been asleep in the garden. But for one who sleeps in prison, it hurts to be awakened.
>
> Practice *samā'* where there is a wedding (with the Divine Attributes), not in a place of wailing or mourning (i.e. mourning the death of the Divine Attributes in people). *Samā'* is not for those who have not seen the substance of their own selves, for from them the moon is hidden. How can *samā'* and the tambourine be suitable for such people, as *samā'* is intended to make possible union with the Beloved?

Dhu'l-Nūn, a sufi master of the ninth century A.D., once said:

> *Samā'* is what descends from God and arises in the hearts of seekers, spiritually empassioning them and increasing their yearning for God. Whoever listens to it selflessly, from God, finds the way to God; whoever listens with self-consciousness, with awareness of self, falls into duality and separation.

Sa'dī, one of the greatest Persian poets and a sufi of the thirteenth century A.D., has written:

> I will not say what *samā'* is unless I know who the listener is. If it is someone who can fly in the spiritual world, *samā'* will cause such a one to fly higher than the angels. But if it is someone who is inclined towards play and amusement, the pull of the worldly self will be strengthened in his being. The world is full of those intoxicated with *samā'*, those totally devoted to the Beloved. But a man who is spiritually deaf will not hear, any more than a blind man will see in a mirror. The morning's breeze will scatter the flower, but an ax is needed to cut up pieces of wood.

Shiblī has said:

> From the outside, *samāʿ* looks like a distraction, but its inner reality is that of guidance. For one who knows its real meaning, it is both a guide and in accordance with religious law. But for the participant who looks at it only outwardly, it is as if he or she is asking for trouble and attached to difficulty.

In other words, *samāʿ* can be a misfortune or a calamity for those whose hearts are not totally drowned in the *samāʿ* of God.

4. Hujwīrī, the author of one of the earliest sufi classics, *Kashf al-maḥjūb*, writes :

> The effect of *samāʿ* can be very different, depending on one's degree of spiritual realization. For the penitent, *samāʿ* brings remorse. For those longing for God, it increases their yearning. For the believers, it strengthens their certainty. For disciples, it verifies what they have been taught. For lovers, it helps to cut their attachments. And for selfless sufis, it is the basis of their loss of 'faith and trust in this world', enabling them to give up everything, including themselves.

5. In *samāʿ*, some benefit more from the meaning of the words and some from the sounds and rhythms. As Junayd has said:

> The hearts of some are in the presence of God; in *samāʿ* these people are helped by the meaning of the words. When the words relate to their states at that time, it is by the meanings that these sufis, completely in the present moment, take part in *samāʿ*. Others hear mainly the sounds and rhythms and pay no attention to the words. For them, the sounds and rhythms are indeed food for the soul. When they receive this food, their states become such that the concerns of the self have been left behind.

6. The gnostics are affected and helped by *samāʿ* in various ways according to their spiritual level. As Rūzbihān has said:

> If the sufis are aware of their spiritual stations while in *samāʿ*, they will experience pain. If they are self-consciously aware of their spiritual states, they will be veiled from God. If they are conscious of listening by God's

> unveiling, they will be in unity. And if they listen by God, to God and in God, it will be true witnessing and they will be in the presence of Divine Beauty.

7. Some sufi shaikhs have said that *samā'* nourishes those who are on the path, but that those who have arrived at the Truth no longer need such nourishment.

Musical Instruments in *Samā'*

Usually, the reed pipe (*ney*) and the tambourine are used in the sufi *samā'*. In the last century, one sufi master, Mushtāq, used to play the four-stringed *sitār*. In sufi poetry, the reed pipe, *daf*, harp, tar, rebeck, lute and tamboura have all been mentioned. In the *Diwān-i Shams-i Tabrīzī*, Rūmī wrote this poem about the *rubāb* (which is the Persian word for rebeck):

The rubāb, *fountain of love,*
companion to the intimates of God,
resembling a rain cloud [indeed the Arabs
call clouds 'rubāb']
which slakes the garden's thirst,
feeds and intoxicates man's spirit.
Blow on coals, you get fire;
blow at dirt, you get dust.
The rubāb *calls back the falcon*
to its royal master,
but even drums will never
fetch the crow.
The rubāb *unties lovers' knots*
if need be,
but those who live like beasts
can do with grass and straw,
sleeping the sleep of desire
and forgetfulness.
You cannot compare a mule
with the loving breath of Jesus;
God has not given mules
the breath that opens doors.
Love, God's gift to the soul,
crown of His Glory,

tears aside the veil and brings union
with the Beloved.
The call of the rubāb
draws all hearts to the One.
The call of God frees them
from their myriad idols.
Do not speak of love
to lovers of self and the world,
those who are pulled and tossed
by fear and hope,
punishment and reward.

The Stations of *Samā'*

In *samā'* there are three stations: understanding, *wajd*, and movement.

1. Understanding

Judged in terms of their understanding of *samā'*, people fall into three groups:

1. Those who practice *samā'* without knowing the path and without constant remembrance of God. Their case is not worth discussing.

2. Those seekers whose minds are occupied with religion (surrender to God) and whose hearts are inclined toward the love of God. They are traveling the spiritual path. Those in this category will experience different states, such as spiritual expansion and contraction, ease and difficulty, and feelings of being accepted or rejected by God. Thus, when the seekers hear in *samā'* ideas of acceptance or rejection, of nearness or separation, fulfillment or unfulfillment and so forth, then whatever is in the seekers' minds and hearts will be intensified and they will thereby experience different states. If one's faith is not strong, if one is not constantly surrendering in the selfless remembrance of God, then one's attention may be diverted towards one's own thoughts and states, and one may fall from the Oneness of God into selfhood and infidelity to the Truth.

As an example, take the seekers on the path who at the beginning progress rapidly, but whose progress then slows down. These people may begin to question whether God is giving them grace any longer. By letting their attention go in this direction, by dwelling on their states and the supposed diminution of God's grace, they have become unfaithful and neglected the moment by moment surrender to God. The thought that God changes is merely an illusion; God is unchanging. It is the seekers who have changed by attending to themselves, by forgetting the Oneness and Reality of God.

3. Finally, there is the *samāʻ* of those who are in the state of 'passing away of the self in God' (*fanā'*). This *samāʻ* is by means of true understanding. When *samāʻ* comes to these people, the states of non-existence and oneness are renewed and freshly overcome them again.

2. Wajd

When a strong yearning for God arises in sufis during *samāʻ*, and they experience various emotions, they are said to be in a state of *wajd*. In the terminology of Sufism, *wajd* is that which, when it reaches the sufis' hearts, causes the sufis to become aware of fear or sadness. It is the unveiling of something from the 'unseen world' to the innermost being, or it is a state between the sufi and God. Sometimes it seems to come from the pain of separation, at other times from a burning love and ardor for God, but usually it is experienced with the pain of separation. When this is felt in the sufis' innermost being and takes charge of them, they may appear disturbed and noises or shouts may come from them. This state is called *wajd*. As Rūzbihān has said:

> Trying to experience *wajd* is permitted only for lovers, not for others. *Wajd* does not come to those whose worldly nature is still alive in them. It is incompatible with anything other than God. Therefore, those who are centered in their worldly selves will not experience *wajd*. It arises directly from the Divine Beauty when God shows one's spirit His Face. A stranger to God will never see such beauty.

Some say that *wajd* descends from the Absolute and arises in the spiritual heart of the true seeker. In its manifestations, it is sometimes experienced as joy, at other times as sadness, thus changing the inner being of the sufi. Perhaps the most beautiful definition of *wajd* is that given by Sumnūn Muḥibb:

> If *samāʻ* is God's call to the soul, *wajd* is the soul's response. Unconsciousness is the result of reaching God, while

> weeping is one of the effects of the joy of experiencing union.

The Various Kinds of *Wajd*

Rūzbihān has said that *wajd* may be of three kinds:

1. Most sufis experience it as an intense burning feeling.
2. The elect know it as complete surrender.
3. For the elect of the elect, it is at one and the same time a state of being conscious of one's separation from the Beloved on the material plane, yet being totally one with the Beloved in the spiritual realm. In explanation of this point, Muḥammad Ghazālī has said:

> There are two kinds of *wajd*: one belongs to the world of spiritual states and the other to the realm of unveiling of the Divine.
>
> The first occurs when yearning, fear, the fire of love, seeking, grief, remorse or some other such quality predominates in the sufis and intoxicates them. When this happens, the heart, mind and senses are all under its spell. In this state, the sufis are asleep to the world, neither seeing nor hearing anything, no more attentive to the world of the senses than if they were drunk.
>
> The second form of *wajd* may come either cloaked in the form of thoughts or directly in an intuitive or contemplated vision. In this state of *wajd*, *samā‘* cleanses and polishes the mirror of the heart until the true nature of Reality appears. Such *wajd* cannot really be explained by scientific arguments, by analogies, or by giving examples. Only those who have experienced it know its reality.

The Levels or Degrees of *Wajd*

1. *Tawājud*—this is the level experienced by people who have not become completely selfless, but are trying to put themselves in that state.
2. *Wajd*—this level of experience is for those who have gone beyond self, but are still aware that they have gone beyond.
3. *Wujūd*—this is the level of those who have not only gone beyond self, but beyond even the awareness of that condition. They have surrendered even the awareness of having given up everything.

The Differences Among These Three Levels of *Wajd*

In Arabic, many words are derived from roots called 'infinitives'. Both *wajd* and *wujūd* are infinitives, the former meaning 'grief' and the latter 'finding'. The active noun for both words is *wājid,* meaning one in a state of *wajd* or *wujūd.* In the terminology of Sufism, *wajd* and *wujūd* are the names of two distinct states experienced in *samā'*. *Wajd* is related to the grief brought on by feeling the loss of the Beloved, as well as the feeling of not having access to Him, while *wujūd* is related to finding the Beloved.

The subtle difference between ordinary sorrow and *wajd* is that sorrow comes when one's attention is on the self, whereas *wajd* is a grief of love that comes when one pays attention to God. The mysteries of *wajd* are hidden from awareness and what is so hidden cannot be written down by the pen. So *wajd* can be regarded as a secret between the seeker and the Sought a secret that others cannot share. Similarly, *wujūd* is grace conferred on the lover by the Beloved—a grace that cannot be explained.

Wajd is a pain that may be felt in the heart as either joy or sadness, but *wujūd* means that the heart is freed of sadness and has reached its Beloved. The attributes of a *wājid* are vigorous involuntary movements coming from the intensity of the yearning for God while remaining veiled from the Beloved, and complete stillness while in the state of unveiling and witnessing.

One day, Junayd was sitting with some other sufi shaikhs when a singer happened to sing a few lines of poetry. The bodies of the other shaikhs began to move in the *wajd* of *samā'*. After a while they asked Junayd, "Have you no share in this *samā*?" In reply, Junayd quoted the Koranic verse, "And you see the hills which you think are so solid. [They are] flying with the flight of the clouds." What he meant here was that he was in *wujūd,* a state of God witnessing God, a state which the other shaikhs could not share.

Wajd then is an attribute of the disciple, while *wujūd* is an attribute of the one who has direct knowledge of God. *Wajd* is the seeker's burning ecstasy, while *wujūd* the Divine gift which God bestows on those whom He loves. One who is in a state of *wajd* has still not gone beyond the last veil of the worldly self. By the very consciousness of one's own existence, one is veiled from God. When a moment comes in which the seeker's consciousness surrenders to the ever-present Oneness of the Beloved, a ray of the light of God will shine upon his or her being; in *wajd* he or she will perceive it. Then, once more, the veil 'will fall' in between and that which was found will be lost again. This is the process of *wajd.* It is a state bridging two states of separation.

The meaning of *wujūd* is that in this state the sufi's consciousness of self becomes totally absent. Thus, *wajd* is an attribute of the temporal, and *wujūd* an attribute of the Eternal. As Dhu'l-Nūn has said:

> *Wujūd* resides in the ever-present Being of God, while *wajd* resides in one who experiences it (i.e. one who experiences *wajd* is still aware of and paying attention to his or her own being. One's 'consciousness of self' has not totally passed away in God, while the 'consciousness of self' of one in a state of *wujūd* has been completely eliminated to the point that one exists and is eternal by the very Reality of God alone).

Therefore, those who still perceive their own *wajd* remain veiled from the state of God witnessing God in God. They experience joy as a result of perceiving their *wajd.* But for those who at every moment allow God's witnessing of God in God to appear, and thus become absent from awareness of themselves and their *wajd*, their joy stops.

Wajd is the beginning of *wujūd.* It is like a boulder-throwing catapult, constructed by the pull of God, by which sufis are ravaged by God. When the catapult time and again hurls its boulders at the walls of the fortress of 'self'-consciousness and finally destroys it, then *wajd* becomes *wujūd.* Thus, the end of *wajd* is the beginning of *wujūd.*

It is said that one day Shiblī was at the peak of a spiritual state when he came to Junayd who at that time was grieving. Shiblī asked, "Dear Shaikh, what has happened?" Junayd replied, "He who seeks (God), grieves." Then Shiblī said, "No, it is the other way around. He who grieves seeks." Both were correct. The former spoke from *wajd*, and the latter from *wujūd.*

Just as *wajd* is the beginning of *wujūd*, so *tawājud* is the beginning of *wajd. Tawājud* is an attempt to put one's self into a state of *wajd* by thinking of union, desiring to be truly God's, and speaking to the heart about witnessing and the riches of God.

Some people, who pay attention only to the superficial, imitate the external movements of those genuinely in *wajd*; this is absolutely forbidden by the Divine Law. However, for others, who are actually seeking God and whose goal is the spiritual states and the realization of the great sufis, *tawājud* is permitted. Rūmī had this to say about *tawājud*:

Samā' is for the restless soul!
Rise up lightly then; this is no place for just
waiting expectantly.
Don't sit here all wrapped up in your thoughts.
If you are truly of God, go where the Beloved is.
Don't say, "Let us wait until the Beloved calls us,"

for how can a thirsty man think like this?
The moth does not think of the fire as he flies
into the flame.
For a soul that loves,
thought is nothing short of disgraceful.

The Meaning of the Cries and Appearances of Those in *Wajd*

Sufi masters have said that *wajd* is the heart's seeing and hearing. In other words, whenever sufis become tired from the trials and tribulations of love, when they see or hear something in *wajd*, their pain is renewed. Then cries, groans and other sounds are torn from them.

One can assess the state of sufis in terms of the sounds and cries that come from them in *wajd*. They may come from joy or from sadness, from fear or devotion, from yearning or from other states. One whose inner state is fearful will externally manifest dread, dumbness and breathlessness. One who is in a state of love will show the signs of unfulfilled desire, while one whose inner state is characterized by intense yearning will manifest bewilderment. In these cases, one's outer condition is called *wajd*, but one's inward condition is a particular spiritual state.

The *Wajd* of Beginners and That of the Advanced

Wajd is a perfection in the spiritual state of the beginner and an imperfection in the spiritual state of the advanced, since it applies to the temporary regaining of a state of God witnessing God. One cannot speak of 'regaining' without having first lost that state:

For the one whose comfort is found in wajd
it brings joy.
But for one who is in a state of God
witnessing God, wajd *does not exist.*

The *wajd* of the seeker takes place only up to the state of *fanā'* (when consciousness of self has fallen away with the coming of the light of God witnessing God), but when the sufi's consciousness is of Oneness, there is no *wajd*. Therefore, whoever experiences *wajd* has lost the state of realizing Absolute Reality. The reason for the loss of the selfless state of God witnessing God in God is that the qualities of existence have manifested themselves. These qualities are of two kinds: of the light and of the dark. To the darkness belong the attributes of the ‘self’. Such qualities are the veils of beginners. To the light, on the other hand, belong the qualities of the heart, which are the veils of the more advanced—those who have surrendered themselves to God to the extent that the veils of their worldly desires and fears have fallen away and only the veils of their spiritual attachments remain.

Some shaikhs have allowed beginners to engage in *tawājud* not for the purpose of reaching a true spiritual state in *wajd*, but simply for comforting the troubled heart and ridding the mind of fatigue. Thus, one can give oneself over to rhythmic movements accompanied by pleasing songs so that for a short time one's ‘self’ will be relieved of the pain and burden of responsibility.

In some cases, those who engage in *tawājud* try to storm the gates of *wajd* by imitating those who really experience it, hoping in this way to draw down upon themselves its spiritual grace. Although this form of *tawājud* is permitted for the beginner, it is of course unsuitable for sufi masters whose inner and outer states are the pure Truth.

Especially when in the presence of a sufi shaikh, sufis should not cry out unless they cannot control themselves. The master of Junayd, Sarī Saqaṭī, has said, “It is permissible for those in *wajd* to cry out and make sounds on the condition that at the instant of the cry, if they were struck on the face by a sword, they would not feel the pain.”

Samā‘ for the spiritually advanced does not induce crying and clamor because these noises happen as a result of God manifesting in such a way that the sufi's consciousness does not fully surrender. Then, the falling away of ‘self’-consciousness is abruptly halted and an involuntary cry comes from the body as he or she is being shocked back into his or her ordinary state. On this point, one of the companions of Sahl ibn ‘Abdullāh Tustarī, a sufi master, has said:

> For years I did not notice any changes in Sahl during *samā‘* until, towards the end of his life, this verse of the Koran was recited in his presence: “So this day no ransom can be taken from you, nor from those who disbelieved. Your home is the fire that is your patron and a hapless journey's end.” With this, his state suddenly changed and he shook so hard that he almost fell down. When I asked him why, he said, “From weakness.”

Errors in *Wajd*

1. Sometimes the deliberate manifestation of the signs of *wajd* is a form of

lying before God. Since the involuntary manifestation of true *wajd* in *samāʿ* is an indication that God has given the sufis a spiritual gift, they are lying before God if they act like they are in *wajd* when really they are not.

2. It is a mistake for people to endanger those present in the *samāʿ* gathering by willfully manifesting signs of a state that they do not really have at the moment. This amounts to a betrayal.

3. It is also a mistake to destroy the trust of those who believe in Sufism, thereby preventing them from receiving spiritual help from other sufis. When some of those present in the *samāʿ* session believe that someone is a true sufi because of the way he or she acts when imitating *wajd*, then afterwards, when he or she does something to upset their belief, they may lose their trust in the truth of Sufism and decide that all sufis behave this way. As a result, their opportunity of receiving help from the sufis may be lost.

Thus, sufis truly in *wajd* do not move until their being is completely overwhelmed in *samāʿ* and movements spontaneously and involuntarily come upon them.

3. Movement (Dancing)

Dancing is not getting up any time painlessly
like a speck of dust blown around in the wind.
Dancing is when you rise above both worlds,
tearing your heart to pieces, giving up your soul.

—Rūmī

ʿIrāqī, a sufi master of the thirteenth century A.D., has written:

> The Beloved, by saying the word "*kun*" ('Be!'), awoke the lover from the sleep of non-existence. Hearing this melody (*samāʿ*), he was overcome by *wajd* and from it received his life. The immediate taste of this melody penetrated his whole mind. Love took over, and at that point, man's complete stillness was transformed into sacred dance and movement. Until eternity without end, neither the melody nor the dance will be completed, for the Beloved is infinite and endless. Thus, the lover is continuously in spiritual movement and dance, even if he seems still.

Sometimes the movement of sufis in *wajd* are like dance movements. This indicates a very advanced degree of *wajd*. When this state comes, passion and yearning for the Beloved take control of the sufis' limbs and bodies. Intoxicated by Divine Love, without awareness of self and without volition, the sufis may stamp their feet on the ground and their hands may clap. This is called the 'Dance of Oneness'.

Neither in the *sharī'at* (which lays down the religious duties of Muslims) nor in the *ṭarīqat* (the spiritual path) is there any basis for dancing. But since the movements of those in *wajd* and the actions of those taking part in *tawājud* resemble dancing, people who have seen only their outer behavior have imitated these movements and even gone further setting up 'spiritual paths and groups' based on them. Often, it is such groups that people have come to think of as representing 'Sufism'.

In true Sufism, the tearing of clothes and all movements and dancing are involuntary. A Persian poet, Khāqānī, has written:

See the falcons who have flown from the nest
of the path (ṭarīqat);
In wajd *they are like homing pigeons, whirling*
and turning.

In the sayings of the Prophet, involuntary movements of *wajd* are recorded as follows:

> It is said that the Prophet once said to 'Alī, "You are of me, and I am of you." When he heard this, 'Alī became ecstatic and involuntarily his feet beat on the ground.
>
> The Prophet once said to Ja'far, the brother of 'Alī, "You are like me in both looks and character." Here again, in *wajd*, Ja'far involuntarily stamped on the ground.

It is recorded that Rūzbihān was once on the roof of a *khānaqāh* while in a state of *wajd*. It happened that a group of young people was passing by in the alley below, playing musical instruments and singing:

O heart, in the neighborhood of the Beloved
there is no wailing,
nor are the roof, door or windows
of Her house guarded.

If you are ready to lose your soul,
get up and come now, for the battlefield
is empty.

When he heard this, Rūzbihān was overcome by an ecstatic state which flung him from the roof, whirling and turning in the air, to the ground below. On witnessing this, the group of young people cast away their instruments, left their former ways, entered the *khānaqāh* and became sufis.

Abū Sa'īd ibn Abī'l-Khayr, a great sufi master of the eleventh century A.D., considered that clapping hands and stamping feet could help young people lessen, at least for a time, the grip of their worldly passions and desires. About this he has said:

> It is in the nature of young people that they are not free of desires. These dominate them and control their bodies. If they clap their hands and stamp their feet, the intensity of their desires will be lessened and they will be better able to control their outward actions. It is better to release some of the excessive intensity of their emotions (in the name of God) in *samā'* than to have to let it out among people, with possible injury to themselves and others.

One of the greatest Persian mystics, Shaikh Suhrawardī, who lived in the thirteenth century A.D., understood the dance of the sufis as a kind of worship, provided it was done with the correct intention. However, he considered it to be religiously prohibited if people were dancing to show off a supposedly ecstatic state.

In any case, *samā'* is not what those who call themselves sufis do in imitating the involuntary and ecstatic movements of real sufis. Nor is it that which is performed by people who go about from city to city selling spirituality to make a living, and who, in order to build up their 'spiritual business', take scorpions' tails between their lips, place the heads of poisonous snakes in their mouths, drive spikes into their bodies, chew rocks and broken glass, and consider these things to be signs of Divine miracles and grace. On this point, Rūmī has written:

These spiritually destitute people that you see,
knowing nothing of the Truth,
only worship themselves. Leave them alone!
They are owls in the ruins that constitute this world,
far removed from the melodies of nightingales.
They have fixed themselves up to look spiritual,

but it is impossible to find a trace
of true spirituality in any of them.

Dancing and movements that are not involuntary, though considered by some people a means of purification and of arriving at Love and Truth, are not the true *samā‘* of the sufis. Dancing as such will not cause anyone to reach the Ocean of Love. Rather, it is one who is already in love, the true lover, who becomes absent from himself or herself and overcome by spontaneous movement and dancing. As Mīr Ḥusaynī Harawī has said:

If they think that their rites,
mannerisms and actions are the method,
Then they have left and forgotten
the way of God's people.

Of course, as noted above, some sufi shaikhs have considered that consciously dancing and moving in *tawājud* could be a way to facilitate liberation by breaking one's resistance to surrendering to the Beloved. In this context, Rūmī has said:

Dance where you can break yourself to pieces
and totally abandon your worldly passions.
Real men dance and whirl on the battlefield;
they dance in their own blood.
When they give themselves up, they clap their hands;
when they leave behind the imperfections
of the self, they dance.
Their minstrels play music from within;
whole oceans of passion foam
on the crest of their waves.

In some cases, the movements of the sufis have a special meaning. On the spiritual path, there are various movements to accompany certain *dhikrs* that are aimed at establishing the selfless remembrance of God in the heart. The purpose of such movements is to harmonize the body with the heart; these movements must be done while one's attention is in and of God, with the corresponding *dhikr*. Among these movements are the whirling of the body and the moving of the neck from side to side. These are well-known and well-understood actions for the sufis, which must be done in private. However, sometimes sufis may become so absent from themselves that the movement corresponding to their *dhikr* will show itself in public. Those who see it may not understand what it really is, and may think it is a form of dancing. Thus, as an example, we may recall the whirling movements of Rūmī while he was in *wajd* and his heart was involved in his *dhikr*. As Aflākī in *Manāqib al-'ārifīn* has written:

> While in a state of being wholly under the influence of *samā'* and his passion for God, Rūmī was walking by the shops of some goldsmiths. Just from the rhythm of the pounding of their hammers, such an intense spiritual passion and ecstasy came upon him that his whole body began to whirl.

Samā' in the Time of Shāh Ni'matullāh

(A Sufi Master of the Fourteenth Century A.D.)

In Shāh Ni'matullāh's time, there were *samā'* sessions that were conducted in accordance with the injunctions of religious law and proper behavior. Some of the characteristics of these sessions were as follows:

1. In the *samā'* sessions of Shāh Ni'matullāh (unlike the ordinary *samā'* gatherings at that time), dancing, whirling and turning were not common.

2. In his sessions, there was hand-clapping and sometimes the playing of the reed pipe and the tambourine, but the other musical instruments of that period were not used.

3. At the beginning of these gatherings, Shāh Ni'matullāh would sit down facing the *qibla*[1]. At his word, those sufis who were present would then turn the attention of their hearts towards the Beloved and would begin their *dhikr*s, usually in the form of *Lā ilāha ill Allāh*, which is usually translated as "(There is) no god but God," or "(There is) no reality but the Reality." During the repetition of the first part of this *dhikr*, '*Lā ilāha*' ('no god'), the sufis moved their heads to the right, signifying 'no', or as it is sometimes called, the action (arc) of negation of possibility. Then, with the saying of '*ill Allāh*' ('but God'), they moved their heads to the left, towards the heart, signifying 'yes', or the action (arc) of affirmation of Necessity.

In whichever direction Shāh Ni'matullāh moved his head, a feeling of expansion and joy would arise in the hearts and souls of those present. At the end of the session, the sufis would prostrate themselves before God, and Shāh Niʿmatullāh would lead them in prayer.

ʿAbd al-ʿAzīz Wāʿizī, one of the biographers of Shāh Niʿmatullāh, has written:

> During the *samāʿ* session, Shāh Niʿmatullāh's state combined that of the intoxicated lover with that of the skilled warrior who has turned away from the world and everything in it, who has become one with the Beloved, witnessing the Beloved in the Beloved.

1 *qibla:* the direction of Mecca, towards which Muslims face when they pray, symbolizing the orientation of the body, the mind and the heart toward God.

Master and Disciple

Stop all this cleverness and planning,
for love closes the gates of the Divine
to the hearts of those who do not
completely lose themselves on the path of devotion.

—Ḥāfiẓ

The terms 'master' and 'disciple' have been much misunderstood in recent years, with the result that, for anyone interested in knowing about the path, a brief clarification is very much in order. This essay will serve to explain the correct behavior and duties involved in this relationship and clear away certain misconceptions that may be held.

While an understanding of this relationship may be interesting to the general public, it is absolutely essential for darvishes, so that the foundation of their spiritual devotion will not become undermined by mistaken or foolish notions of behaving or being.

An erroneous approach may cause a disciple to undo many years of struggle on the path, or to waste an entire lifetime without ever picking a flower from the garden of love and devotion or inhaling the fragrance of the Truth. For this reason, I have prepared this essay and made it available to the friends and seekers of God. May it help to serve, guide and enlighten those who are truly seeking and yearning for the Truth.

The Master

There would be no movement in the stars,
nor any stillness at the axis of the universe
were there no human beings on earth.

—Ḥāj Mullā Hādī Sabzavārī

The master (*murād*, lit. 'the desired one') is a person who guides travelers on the path of 'passing away of the self in God' (*fanā' fi'llāh*) and leads them towards subsistence in God (*baqā' bi'llāh*).

The master is called by different names according to varying characteristics. For example:

'Shaikh'—As regards the depth of the true knowledge of God that he or she possesses, he or she is among the great sufis.

'Pīshvā'—The leader of seekers on the path of the eternal Truth.

'Murshid' and 'Hādī'—The guide and sustainer of travelers on the spiritual path.

'Bāligh'—The manifestation of the perfection of true maturity, the Divine Attribute of 'Being Human'.

'The Perfect Human Being'—The perfect realization of all of the Divine Attributes.

'The Mirror that reflects the universe' and *'the Goblet that reveals the world'* —The master is a mirror reflecting entirely the Perfect Human Being, who is the complete manifestation of the whole of creation. He or she embodies the fullness of Divine perfection, and in his or her face the vicegerency of God is manifested.

'The Great Cure'—The master cures those who are afflicted with Divine Love, heals the wounds of those whose hearts are burned, and aids those who have lost their hearts.

'The Sublime Elixir'—The master transmutes the copper of seekers' hearts into pure gold and cleanses their being.

'Jesus'—By the breath of the Holy Spirit, the master resurrects those who have died on the way of love, cures those whose souls are in deep pain and, when necessary, sacrifices his or her life for humanity.

'Enoch', 'Elias' or 'Elijah' (Persian, Khiḍr)—The master has drunk of the water of life and, until post-eternity, lives by love. In the darkness of the way to the Truth, he or she lights the lamp that shows travelers how to be.

'Solomon'—The master understands the language of those who travel on the path, as did Solomon, who understood the language of the birds, and is able to communicate with each traveler in his or her own language.

'Noah'—The master is like a stable mountain in the midst of the storm raging on the surface of the Ocean of Reality, saving voyagers from the whirlpools of destruction and guiding them to the ark of deliverance and fulfillment.

'Elder' (pīr)—The master has great experience, having tasted the warmth and coldness of the way of love.

'Master of the Winehouse' (pīr-i maykada)—The master understands the intoxicated state of drunkards on the path, a state that comes from having drunk deeply from the cup of love. He or she pours for each a chalice of the wine of difficulty, filling it according to the heart's deepest desire. The master guides to peace those who have become drunk and agitated and brings a goblet of the wine of love to those who have not yet imbibed, giving them a taste of ecstasy and rapture.

'Master of the Holy Fire' (pīr-i mughān)—The master lights a holy flame in the hearts of novices on the path and, knowing the secrets of hearts, trains each person on the spiritual path according to his or her ability to understand.

'Master of the Tavern of Ruin' (pīr-i kharābāt)—The master knows the secrets of the 'Tavern of Ruin', the spiritual station of the passing away of the self in God, and sees the light of God everywhere.

'Axis of the Universe' (quṭb)—The master is a perfect human being and the axis around which the world of Divine Knowledge and spiritual realization revolves.

Some Attributes of the Master

The master is incomparably exalted. He or she is the object of God's constant attention, and his or her being is completely comprised of Divine Attributes. The master knows the essence of Reality and has polished the tarnish of multiplicity from the mirror of his or her heart. The master has journeyed to the end of the way of spiritual poverty and abandonment of self. He or she is the guide of the spiritual path and the sun of the Truth.

The master is the Noah of the ark of the voyagers of purity and the basis of illumination and revelation for those who are faithfully carried away by the spiritual wind. The master takes the hands of stragglers who have fallen behind and leads them onwards, while enabling those who are well advanced to arrive at the Truth. The master liberates travelers from the dark night of self-worship and brings them into the brilliance of that clear daylight, which in this world is the paradise of the selfless witnessing of the Divine Truth.

I am a disciple of the master of the holy fire.
O preacher, do not be displeased with me.
For the master has fulfilled in this world
What you have but promised in the next.

—Ḥāfiẓ

The attention of the master is an elixir that transmutes the copper hearts of travelers to gold and delivers them from the brink of disaster. The master burns away the lovers' existence and illuminates them by the light of the Beloved.

By a glance we transform dust into gold,
and by a flash from the corner of one eye,
we cure a hundred pains.

—Shāh Ni'matullāh

The robe of the master is the robe of the Prophet:[1]

No matter what part of the world
the masters are from,
in soul and body,
they are of the Prophet's line.
It matters not where a rose grows:
it is still a rose;
wherever a vat of grapes ferments,
there is wine.
If the sun rises in the west,
it is still the sun.
Whatever the master possesses,
whether worldly goods or spiritual qualities,
is entrusted to his successor.
That is why in every era
a master arises,
and this Divine experiment
will continue until the end of time.

—Rūmī

Though totally and utterly needy, the master lacks nothing. Far from the world of illusion, he or she is one with the Absolute Truth.

Though solitary and alone,
the master is a King
Whose armies and servants
are his spiritual intent and all-consuming love.

—Rūmī

For the master there is no multiplicity, only the One. There is no one to help him or her except the One.

Those who know the soul are freed
from the bonds of multiplicity,
for they have been drowned
in the dimensionless Ocean of Oneness.
In the heart of grapes,

they see wine,
in the passing away of all,
they see the world as it really is.
Though in appearance human,
in essence they are Gabriel, the Holy Spirit,
freed from anger and desire
and the nonsense of words.

—Rūmī

The Master from the Viewpoint of the Koran

It is necessary to bear in mind that the banquet of love is not suitable for everyone; such a blessing is not given to those who are ensnared in the desires of the self.

As regards the master, God has said, "...a slave of My slaves, I have given him Divine Mercy from nearness to Me, and taught him Divine Knowledge directly from Me" (Koran 18:65).

In this Koranic verse, God clarifies the five qualities of a spiritual master. The first quality is termed that of being a chosen slave and arises from the reference, "...a slave of My slaves..." Such a chosen slave of God is one who is freed from the delusion that there could be anything other than God.

The beggar at Your door
does not need the eight gardens of Paradise.
The prisoner of Your love
is freed from this world and the next.

—Ḥāfiẓ

The second quality of mastery arises from the ability to perceive the realities of being directly from Reality. This is expressed in the phrase, "...I have given him Divine Mercy..." No one is worthy of such a spiritual station unless completely freed from the layers and layers of veils that form the differentiations of Absolute Reality into the relative levels of being (that is, the spiritual planes and the material world). For until one is freed from veils, everything that emanates from behind the veils will appear with the veil as an intermediary reflection, and will be distorted accordingly, taking on the characteristics of that particular veil or plane of being.

The third quality of mastery concerns the Grace of nearness to God and is expressed by the phrase, "...Mercy from nearness to Me..." The results of this Mercy comprise the illumination of the Divine Attributes, the effacement of all human qualities, and the acquisition of Divine ways of being.

The fourth quality of mastery results from the honor of receiving Divine Wisdom from the realm of the Absolute Reality, as expressed in the phrase, "...and I have taught him..." Unless the tablet of the heart becomes cleansed of the forms and images of relative knowledge, it will not be able to accept the inscription of the Truth; in other words, the disciple will not be ready to receive Divine Knowledge and become a master.

The fifth quality of mastery consists of an awareness of Divine Knowledge that is received directly from God, without any intermediary and is expressed in the phrase, "...Divine Knowledge directly from Me..."

Therefore, if someone is really a master, his or her being must include the five qualities described above:

Not every illumined face
knows how to be a beloved one,
nor do all those who make mirrors
see the universe reflected in them
as did Alexander.[2]
Not everyone who puts on a crown
and sits upon a throne
knows how to be a king.
Here are a thousand fine points,
narrower than a single hair, for
not everyone who shaves his head
is as free as the qalandars.[3]

—Ḥāfiẓ

The Disciple

Take a step towards love,
for on this journey,
There is much to be gained.

Devotion comes from a ray of light emanating from the Attribute of God termed 'being devoted'. Unless God illuminates this Attribute in the slave, unless the reflection of the light of devotion appears in the heart, he or she will not become a devotee. In the Koran, God says, "O Prophet, you do not guide those whom you love; it is God who guides those whom He wills and He knows best those who receive guidance" (28:56).

Indeed, if it is not God's will,
how can one enjoy the fruits of God?

The disciple is a lover whose heart is languishing and weary. He or she is one who has passed beyond both worlds and become united with the Truth. Such a one seeks God alone and in his or her words there is only talk of God. The disciple approaches the Beloved and is ensnared by love. He or she continually purifies the mirror of the heart from the tarnish of 'self', and, through the grace of God, it shines brilliantly.

The disciple is a sincere seeker who is freed from all attachments. The disciple longs for God as he or she passes from 'self' and takes to the path not speaking of self. Such a one has no tale to tell about his or her 'I', and can never complain about the Beloved.

This kingdom of longing
is not given to just anyone,
Nor is this ocean of sadness
entrusted to all hearts and souls.
Those who wish to be healed
are deprived of this gift of torment,
And it is never entrusted
to those who seek a cure.

Abū 'Uthmān Ḥīrī has said, "The disciple is one whose heart has died to everything except God. The disciple longs only for God, and for nearness to God. In the rapture and intensity of Divine Love and passion, the desires of 'self' vanish from the heart."

In an orgy where a thousand souls are sacrificed,
there is no place for itinerant drummers.

Shaikh Abū 'Abdullāh ibn Khafīf has said, "Devotion draws the heart to the Beloved. Its essence is continual effort and abandonment of ease."

You must leave yourself behind,
you must pass from body and soul.
With each step a thousand bonds appear;
a swift traveler is needed, one able to break bonds.

Abū 'Alī Rūdbārī has said, "The disciple wishes for only that which God desires. The master wants nothing from both worlds except God. Thus, the disciple surrenders the self and is content with whatever the Beloved wishes."

The Necessity of Having a Master

In love's domain, do not take
even one step without a guide.
For on this road, one who has no guide
will lose the way for sure.

—Ḥāfiẓ

Create an elixir from a handful of dust
and kiss the doorstep of a perfect being.

—Rūmī

After the seed of the blessing of devotion has fallen into the fertile soil of the heart by the Grace of God, one must not let it wither. Rather, one must place it in the care of a perfect master whose dominion is the entire universe.

In this way, it will be protected from the many ways in which it can be destroyed. This enables the seed to mature and bear fruit in accordance with its innate ability. It is in reference to this that the following Koranic verse was revealed, "O Prophet, guide those who seek the straight path."

The reason why you are so dead and withered
is that you have abandoned the master.
In the ocean of the soul, it is impossible to swim;
here the only salvation is Noah's Ark.
And so, the king of the Prophets declared:
"I am the Ark in this infinite Ocean,

As are those who truly are my successors,
who truly have my Divine vision."
Together we are Noah's Ark in the Ocean,
so do not turn away from this ship!

—Rūmī

If one comes to a master, and one's self-worshipping ego begins to criticize and make excuses, such as, "Is this master perfect or not?", one should remember that "even if a lowly slave speaks, listen carefully and obey." One should bear in mind that it is better to be possessed by another than by one's own self.

Do not say that the Beloved has left
and the City of Love is empty.
The world is full of perfect masters,
but where are the sincere disciples?

—Kamāl Khujandī

Moses, although he was a prophet, served as a disciple. As Ḥāfiẓ wrote, "Moses found the Beloved only after he had served sincerely for a few years." Then, having gained the spiritual riches of prophethood, he was graced, as is described in the following verse: "We wrote on the tablets counsel concerning all things and an explanation of everything" (6:145). With humility, Moses asked his master, Khiḍr, "May I follow you so that you can teach me whatever you have learned about arriving at Reality?" The answer he received was, "You cannot be sufficiently patient with me" (18:67).

The masters of the path have declared the following about the necessity of having a master, "One who has no spiritual master has no religion."

If you do not have a lock
of the Beloved's tresses in your hand,
You are less than a Zoroastrian slave,
as you do not even have his belt of faith.

—From *Suḥbat-i Lārī*

In addition to what has been said above, a number of other reasons exist why a seeker and traveler of the path must have a master.

1. It is not possible for someone to arrive at the Ka'ba of this world without a guide. It is clear, therefore, that to undertake the pilgrimage to the true inner Ka'ba of the heart, one must have a perfect guide, a master who is united with the Beloved.

If you had been without a guide
on that path you traveled many times,
You would have lost your way.
So, do not spurn a guide and venture alone
on that road that you have not yet seen.

—Rūmī

Imām Ja'far Ṣādiq has said, "One who journeys far from the city seeks a guide. You, who are even more ignorant of the celestial than the terrestrial realm, must seek a guide for yourself."

2. As there are many obstacles and traps on the path, the road is extremely dangerous without the Divine grace of a master.

Do not travel through these stations
without the company of a perfect master.
There is darkness. Beware of the danger
of getting lost!

—Ḥāfiẓ

3. The seeker will encounter many trials and difficulties while traveling along the path. It is only through the grace of an enlightened master that he or she will be able to pass through them.

Deadly poison looks like honey and milk.
Wait! Do not journey without a master who knows.

—Rūmī

4. There are many hazards, doubts and mistakes on this journey, so it needs

to be traveled with the help of a master. One can only be liberated from the deceptions of the self by the grace of a perfect guide, who is truly a place of refuge.

Choose a master, for without one
the road on this journey is
full of hazards, fear and danger.
If the shadow of the master is not near,
you will be terrified
by the shrieks of ghouls.

—Rūmī

5. To be cured of the disease of 'self', the sufi needs a spiritual doctor. In this way, by the grace of the master's holy spirit, the sufi's sickness is treated, and his or her pains are cured.

Screaming, wailing, "I am sick,"
how long will you continue to consult
those who are ill themselves?
Seek a doctor who is healthy,
as he can provide a cure
for all the illnesses of the world.

6. The traveler may be overcome by a spiritual state that liberates him or her from the cloak of being human and the garments of water and earth. Here, a ray of light from the Divine Attributes unites with the traveler and the taste of "I am the Truth" may appear.

A danger at this point is that the traveler may fall into pride and imagine that God has descended into and united with him or her. In such cases, a clear-sighted shaikh and capable master is necessary to bring the traveler out of this illusion by spiritual means. If this does not happen, the condition of being lost and off the path can be disastrous.

Imagine that I am wiser than Plato
and that I know by heart the sacred books
of all nations.

I am unfaithful unless I have learned
the secrets of spiritual intimacy
from the master of the path.

—From *Suḥbat-i Lārī*

7. For those who are truly traveling on the spiritual path, witnessings occur. Some of these indicate spiritual progress, while others show imperfections. The master must be informed of these witnessings in order to interpret them properly for the disciple. If the witnessing is truly an indication of spiritual progress, it can be a reason for encouraging the disciple. But if the witnessing indicates imperfection, the master informs the disciple of this, so that the disciple can try to remove it. As those who are of the unseen world know the language of the invisible world, they can truly interpret these secrets of intimacy.

8. Only by the grace, attention, and training of the master will the self-seeing and self-serving nature of the traveler pass away.

Only the master's love
kills the self.
Do not let go of your devotion
to the one who kills the self.

—Rūmī

The Master's Responsibilities to the Disciple

When the possessor of Divine riches accedes to the throne of guidance and dominion and rises in order to guide seekers, he or she of necessity fulfills the responsibilities of a master and observes the way and manners of a beloved one.

Briefly, the master's responsibilities are as follows:

1. The master must be one who knows the laws and doctrine of Islam sufficiently well so that if disciples need to be instructed in such knowledge, the master can teach them, or else refer them to one who is better versed in such matters.

2. The master must be one who has an occupation, so he or she can encourage the disciple to have one as well.

3. To the extent that he or she is able to do so, the master must be one who meets the financial needs of the disciples in order to enable them to undertake the journey to the Truth.

4. The master must not be one who is concerned with people's adverse criticism, so that he or she can protect the disciples from envious and malevolent tongues.

We are not influenced by anyone,
as the hearts of those who have left the world
are set free.

—Ḥāfiẓ

5. The master must not be too involved in worldly affairs and must also not be concerned with the disciple's wealth, as such behavior can easily ruin the beginner's spiritual state of devotion and result in him or her becoming critical. This is essential because a disciple tends to get lost in questioning and criticism at the beginning, and there is no greater disaster for a disciple than that of criticizing the states and behavior of the master.

I am a slave of one who is free
from all possible attachments in the universe.

—Ḥāfiẓ

6. The master must be one who is compassionate with the disciples, not giving them work beyond their capacity, and must prepare them for the path gradually and with loving care.

We are not of those who fell trees;
they are of another kind.
Although we have a hundred axes,
we do not break even one fruitless branch.

—Waḥshī Bāfqī

7. If the master sees that a disciple has made a mistake, he or she neither becomes angry with nor upsets the disciple. Instead, the master may admonish the darvish in a suitable manner at the proper time. Otherwise, it is possible that the disciple will lose devotion to the master.

O Solomon, while you are among
both partridges and falcons,
Maintain a Divine forbearance,
and live peacefully with all birds.
Do not tear the feathers
from the talkative nightingale,
And keep far apart
the unharmonious falcon and crow.

—Rūmī

8. If from human nature, the disciple acts in an unsuitable manner, the master must be able to overlook such misbehavior.

See the kind nature of the tavern master!
Everything we rowdy drunkards do,
to his eyes, is beautiful.

—Ḥāfiẓ

9. The master must not be one who is quick-tempered because the disciple must learn from the master to develop a pleasant disposition. As it is said, "The disciple's inner self is a mirror of the master's actions and manners."

10. The master is one who places the disciple's welfare before his or her own, ensuring the disciple's peace and tranquillity. The master must always keep in mind the following verse from the Koran: "They prefer the welfare of the refugees to their own, though they themselves are needy" (39:9).

11. The master is one whose trust in God is such that he or she never becomes anxious over providing the disciple's sustenance.

When we arrayed ourselves with resolution,
we needed a helmet of Divine intention

And a coat of mail
formed of trust in God.

—Majdhūb-i Tabrīzī

12. The master must be one who receives the rays of Divine bounty and sainthood, so that he or she can transmit them to the disciple. This also enables the master to guide worthy travelers and teach them the remembrances of God.

13. The master must be one who is neither gladdened by an increase of disciples nor saddened by their decrease. He or she knows that each disciple who becomes joined to the master has been brought by God and has come to serve Him. Similarly, the master knows that each disciple who leaves is taken away by this same Reality.

He who acquires false knowledge,
cries out when his listeners leave...
He seeks knowledge to procure students,
not to be liberated from this world.

The master's only customer is God ,Who draws him up
and buys the souls of the true believers...
So leave behind the penniless buyer,
for what can a piece of clay purchase?

—Rūmī

14. The master must be one who does not spare any effort in training disciples. Whether they accept or reject the master's teaching, whether they realize the Truth or die without it, the master is satisfied and not critical of what has been decreed from pre-eternity.

15. The master must be one who in his or her daily life with disciples is always dignified and worthy of respect. Nothing in the master's manner should provide any occasion for the disciple to become rude or flippant. Flippancy on the part of the disciple only weakens his or her devotion to the master, leading such a one away from the path.

16. The master must be one who does not advance the disciple too quickly

on the path. Instead, the master brings the disciple along slowly so that the disciple does not fall away from the path because he or she has been pushed too hard.

17. The master must be one who keeps his or her word to the disciple, even when the disciple is not constant in his or her service or devotion. The master neither neglects his or her duties towards the disciple nor withdraws grace with every mistake the disciple makes.

18. The master must be one who has an august presence. This inspires respect in the disciple's heart and brings about the proper manner in darvishes. The master's majesty and saintliness break down the disciple's 'self', so that peace enters his or her heart. The Satan of 'self'-consciousness loses all power in the presence of such saintliness.

19. The master must be one who sees both millionaires and beggars in the same light. In the master's presence, social position, parentage and wealth are of no importance. Thus, the ground of devotion is kept fertile for the disciple, regardless of his or her standing in the material world.

The Disciple's Duties to the Master

When a sick person recognizes a doctor, or when a disciple has found his or her master and has begun to lose the 'self' in the way of love, that disciple must become familiar with the appropriate behavior and responsibilities. Thus, the disciple will be able to satisfy the master and come into harmony with the will of God, having overcome a major obstacle on the path.

If disciples cannot undertake their responsibilities with respect to the master, they will surely not be able to do so for God. As the sufis have said, "One who spoils the relationship with the lord who is near will not be able to reach the Lord on high."

The master is a lion
and hunting is his work,
while the rest of creation
are but scavengers.
As long as you are able,

try your best to satisfy the master.
Then he will be strong
and active in his hunting.

—Rūmī

The disciple's responsibilities are many and varied. Below are listed some of these duties and the ways in which they must be performed.

1. Disciples must be sincere in their intention and pure in faith. They must realize that the master is a Divine physician who, merely from the disciple's appearance, can perceive the hidden diseases of his or her heart and faith. As it is recorded in the sayings of the Prophet, "They are those who spy upon hearts; therefore, be sincere while sitting with them." In other words, they have access to people's hearts and know their innermost secrets.

The master who sees by the light of God
is aware of the beginning and the end.
He is like a thought
that comes into the heart,
And therein the secret
of one's state is revealed to him.
He who travels throughout the Universe
has no difficulty walking upon the earth.

2. Disciples must take only the master as their guide because if they imagine another person to be more perfect, then the relationship of Divine Love and spiritual intimacy with the master will be weakened, and the master's words and states will cease to produce their proper effect.

3. Disciples must keep the master's secrets. That is, when they become aware of a miracle, some extraordinary power, or some occurrence that the master has kept hidden, they must not divulge it.

Those who know the Truth,
when they have drunk
From the goblet
of true mysteries,

Do not disclose it.
He who can learn the unseen secrets
can keep silent.

—Rūmī

4. Disciples must be silent in the presence of the master and not draw attention to themselves. If they wish to speak, they must do so in accordance with the Koranic verse, "O you who believe, do not speak louder than the Prophet" (49:2).

Take refuge in silence!
If you are seeking a sign,
do not reveal yourself.
When you arrive at the edge
of the Ocean, sit in silence.
Do not consider yourself
the signet in the ring.
It is a mistake for those
who can foresee the future
to proclaim such news.
This only shows
their ignorance and imperfection.

—Rūmī

5. Under no circumstances should disciples seek precedence for themselves over the master. They should keep in mind the following story:

> There was a time when a crowd of people was in the presence of the Prophet. Whenever someone asked him a question, a number of people would express their opinion before the Prophet answered. The following Koranic verse was then revealed, correcting such self-serving behavior: "O you who have kept the faith, do not precede God and the Prophet" (49:1).

6. Both in their inner being and outward manner, disciples must not criticize the master's words or actions. If the master's meaning is not immediately clear, they must wait patiently. If disciples cannot understand the master's words or actions, they must attribute this to their own ignorance, not to any

imperfection in the master. Otherwise, their devotion to the master may lessen. As Moses' master told him, "If you follow me, do not question me about anything until I bring it up" (18:70).

When you find a master, become surrendered;
like Moses, place yourself in the hands of Khiḍr.
O you who are sincere, wait patiently
for the results of the master's guidance.
Then Khiḍr will not say to you,
"Go away! Leave me!"
Anyone who obeys the orders of the master
is liberated from darkness, and becomes illuminated.
Be obedient, like Ishmael before Abraham,
and with joy give up your soul before the blade.
Listen happily, whether the master speaks to you
warmly or with coldness.
Then you will be freed from the bonds
of opposites and the depths of hell.
The master's anger and kindness
are the thunderstorms and sunshine
of life's new spring.
From them grows forth the rose
of the disciple's purity.

—Rūmī

One of Junayd's disciples once asked him a question and then criticized the master's answer. At that point, Junayd said, "If you do not have faith in me, then you must depart."

7. Disciples must not try to test the master, as it is sheer ignorance to imagine that one who is imperfect could influence a Perfect Human Being.

If a disciple tests a master
who is the leader and guide,
That one is but an ass. O you
of little faith!
If you test the master,
it is really you that is being tested.
Testing the master

implies a desire to affect him.
Go away! Do not seek
to influence such a king.
Since you have no true discrimination,
test yourself and think not of others.

—Rūmī

8. In the presence of the master, disciples must abandon all pride, self-esteem and attempts to attract attention. Rather, they must strive to show humility, spiritual poverty and need.

In the presence of Joseph, the beloved,
do not flirt and display your beauty.
Do nothing but cry and weep in supplication
like Jacob, the lover.

—Rūmī

9. Disciples must always place the master's peace and tranquillity before their own.

10. Disciples must keep in mind the Koranic verse, "I will show My path to those who struggle towards Me" (29:69). They must relate this saying to their service and devotion to the master, and to the awaited arrival at the threshold of the Truth. To the fullest extent of their capabilities, disciples must try to serve the master and surrender themselves to the master's spiritual dominion. This involves sparing neither their possessions nor their souls. In such a manner, the disciples' fire of devotion will blaze more fiercely.

If anyone wishes to enter your domain,
O bewitching source of my torment,
The first step is made
by sacrificing one's head.

11. Disciples must not display their knowledge before the master, nor the results of their experience in meditation, as this is but an affirmation of self-worship and a denial of the love of God.

12. Disciples must not speak of worldly affairs or those involved with them

in the presence of the master and thus waste the master's time with useless chatter. If the disciples wish to speak, they must be discreet and sense the right moment to do so. Before speaking, they must seek from God the grace of proper behavior. Having done so, they may then begin to speak.

13. Disciples must not feel that the master is indebted to them because of their devotion. Rather, they must understand that they owe the master everything, as they receive from him or her spiritual expansion, nourishment and Divine Grace. As is said in the Koran (49:17):

> O Prophet, they feel that you are indebted to them, as they have surrendered (accepted Islam). Say to them, 'Do not feel that Islam is indebted to you; on the contrary, if you are sincere, you will know that you are indebted to God because He has guided you to faith.'

14. Disciples must not expect the master to take them by the hand and raise them to the vast expanse of the Transcendental Reality of the Truth. They must be content with whatever state they are in at any given moment, understanding that they will arrive at whatever state they are capable of realizing.

15. Disciples must have jobs, thereby freeing themselves from dependence on the master for their financial support. In this way, they will also not become parasites on other people.

16. If the master expels a disciple, he or she should not go far away but persist in remaining nearby, realizing that grace is received by attending to and serving the master.

By the master's accepting and rejecting of disciples, by testing them in a multitude of ways, disciples are both shown to themselves and known by the master. In such circumstances, many a heart has cried out, "I will either die on the Beloved's threshold or reach the goal."

As an example, Abū 'Uthmān Ḥīrī once went to Nishapur to see Abū Ḥafṣ Ḥaddād and became spiritually enraptured with him. He wished to stay, but Abū Ḥafṣ drove him away and told him not to come back. Abū 'Uthmān Ḥīrī dug a trench at the entrance to the master's house and remained there in the hope that Abū Ḥafṣ might give him permission to re-enter. When Abū Ḥafṣ saw the sincerity and devotion of Abū 'Uthmān, he accepted him as his disciple and treated him with great loving-kindness. Later, Abū 'Uthmān became the closest companion of Abū Ḥafṣ, married his daughter, and eventually succeeded him as master.

17. Disciples must never undertake any matter of consequence without first obtaining permission from the master. They must realize that even though their own opinions may be correct, as long as they are under the guidance of the master, they must not rely upon their own ideas for directing themselves.

18. Disciples must always follow the directions of the master. Although the master is tolerant, patient and forgiving, disciples must not take his or her instructions lightly, for disobedience to the master will adversely affect the disciple's progress.

19. Disciples must consult the master in regard to any witnessings they may have, whether visions or dreams. They must not attempt to evaluate such occurrences on their own, since their source may have been the 'self'. By themselves, disciples may misjudge their validity and misinterpret them. This could be detrimental to them. Thus, they should tell any witnessing to the master, who, with true insight, will be aware of the validity of the witnessing and give its correct interpretation to the disciple.

20. Disciples must diligently listen and be wholeheartedly receptive to the words of the master. They must at all times await with eagerness whatever the master may say, for it is through the master that they receive the words of the Truth.

Because they know with certainty that the master speaks by the inspiration of God and not by the promptings of the self's desires, disciples constantly strive to understand the relationship between their own states and the words of the master. Gradually they will come to feel that they have reached the threshold of the Truth, where they will obtain what is best for them according to their capacity.

21. Disciples must not be too familiar, in either words or actions, in the presence of the master, as this can veil the Divine Majesty and cut off the outpouring of Grace. By being discreet and respectful in the master's presence, the disciple remains receptive to the Divine.

Once a group of disciples who wished to see the Prophet gathered at the door of his house and cried out "O Muḥammad, come out to us." At this point, the following Koranic verses were revealed:

> Those who call you from outside your house know not what they do. It would be better that they wait patiently until you come out. God is most forgiving and compassionate. (49:4-5)

Respect is also shown by not praying in front of the master. In addition, when disciples pray together, or when they are gathered for the *dhikr*, they must control themselves as much as possible, refraining from voluntary bodily movement and crying out. They must also never laugh loudly while in the master's presence.

22. When disciples ask the master a question, it must not be one that is beyond their capacity to understand. Disciples must realize their limits and not ask questions about matters that are beyond their spiritual states and stations. They must realize that the only profitable talk for them to hear is that which is in accordance with their own understanding.

23. Disciples must tell the master their secrets, as well as all the graces and spiritual powers that God may grant them. This is essential because concealing a secret from the master is like tying a knot in one's inner being. This knot closes the way by which spiritual expansion and help is received from the master. However, when the secret has been divulged to the master, the knot becomes untied.

24. When disciples are talking to someone else about the master, they must speak in accordance with the listener's capacity to understand. That is, a disciple should not speak of any matter that the listener will not be able to follow. When a listener does not understand what has been said about the master, he or she cannot profit from what is being said. In such a case, it is possible that the listener's idea of the master will be weakened or even completely undermined.

1 Each master receives the robe of his or her predecessor, which is the sign of his or her assuming the responsibility of being a master. Whoever receives this robe resides at the very threshold of God.

2 Alexander the Great was said to possess a mirror that showed him the whole universe.

3 *qalandars*: sufis who have given up all their attachments and shave their heads as a symbol of spiritual rebirth.

Principles of the Path

O darvish, human beings of every nation and religion all exist by the honorable cloak of existence; all are human beings like you. If you are truly a lover of Absolute Being, then love all beings and be kind to them. By doing so, you prove that you deserve the privilege of belonging to the human family.

O darvish, disrespect for what others hold sacred only indicates your own imperfection. In this regard, try to make yourself perfect in the eyes of those who truly see.

O darvish, you have entered your name in the book of outstanding human beings. If you are incapable of becoming one of these people, at least try not to disgrace those few who truly hold the good name of 'sufi'.

O darvish, if others behave badly towards you, do not consider them to be bad. Rather, look upon them as having a sickness and be kind to them. If you conduct yourself in this way, you truly possess health of the spirit.

There are four principles that the darvishes of the Nimatullahi Sufi Order should put into practice: remembrance (*dhikr*); contemplation (*fikr*); meditation (*murāqiba*); and self-examination (*muḥāsiba*).

Remembrance

The Heart of Sufi Practice

He is the Rememberer and the Remembered.

Happiest were the times spent with the Beloved;
the rest were vain and fruitless.

—Ḥāfiẓ

The Meaning of *Dhikr*

Dhikr is defined in the dictionary as 'remembrance'. According to the sufis, however, this term has a much more specific meaning: total and uncompromised attention to God, ignoring all that is not God.

You remember Us truly in your heart and soul,
only when you have forgotten both the worlds.

—Shāh Niʿmatullāh

Confirming this view is the Koranic passage, "Remember your Lord when you are forgetful ..." (18:24). Although this passage has been interpreted to mean, "Remember your Lord when you are forgetful... of Him," some masters have said that its true interpretation is, "You remember your Lord only when you have forgotten everything else." According to Imām Ja'far Ṣādiq:

> Remembering repentance at the time of remembering God is forgetting the remembrance of God. To truly remember God is to forget all that is other than God, for God has priority over the sum of all things.
>
> (cited by 'Aṭṭār in *Tadhkirat al-awliyā'*)

The sufi text, *Sharḥ-i Ta'arruf,* states, "The true meaning of *dhikr* is to forget everything other than the Remembered." And Khwāja 'Abdullāh Anṣārī has written, "*Dhikr* is freeing oneself from negligence and forgetfulness."

It has also been said that *dhikr* is sitting and waiting for acceptance by the Divine after detachment from humanity. To put it in another way, the sign of a lover is the constant remembrance of the Beloved.

Aḥmad Khaḍrūya was asked, "What is the sign of being a lover?" He replied, "There should be nothing of the two worlds that is greater in one's heart than the remembrance of the Beloved."

Dhikr in the Koran

Many verses occur in the Koran about *dhikr*. Among them are the following:

> Turn away from the one who turns his back on remembrance of Us, who seeks only the life of this world. (53:29)
>
> When you are not in prayer, remember God standing and sitting and lying down. (4:103)
>
> Remember your Lord's Name and devote yourself to Him whole-heartedly. (73:8)
>
> Remember your Lord over and over; exalt Him at daybreak and in the dark of the night. (3:40)
>
> Remember the Name of your Lord in the morning and in the evening. (76:25)

O you who believe, remember God again and again. (33:41)

Remember God over and over; thus may you be successful. (62:10)

Verily, prayer restrains one from evil, and certainly the remembrance of God is greatest. (29:45)

Traditions of the Imams Concerning the Inculcation of *Dhikr*

It is related that the Prophet of Islam once gathered a group of the elect companions privately into a house. He then spoke about the basic *dhikr* of Islam, *Lā ilāha ill Allāh* ('There is no god but God'), asking them to repeat it aloud with him. When this was done three times, he raised his hands, crying, "O God, did this pass Your approval?" After a moment's pause, he told the companions, "Good tidings to you that God blesses you" (*Mirṣād al-'Ibād*). From that time forth, sufi masters have followed the Prophet's example of inculcating *dhikr* in their disciples.

'Alī once asked the Prophet to show him the shortest and easiest path to God. The Prophet told him to recite the *dhikr* of God in solitude. 'Alī asked, "How should I practice *dhikr*?" The Prophet said, "Close your eyes and listen to me saying *Lā ilāha ill Allāh*." 'Alī listened to the Prophet repeat the *dhikr* three times; then the Prophet listened to 'Alī say it three times in return. (*Jawāhir-i Khamsa*)

Thus, many sufi masters maintain that each *dhikr* handed down to their disciples comes through a chain of initiation originating with the Prophet and 'Alī.

The Kinds of *Dhikr*

One can recite the words of *dhikr* heard from anyone, but *dhikr* itself can be bestowed only by a perfect master. To receive *dhikr* in the first manner is like catching a seed scattered by the wind. As Rūmī has expressed it:

You may know this existence is a trap,
yet dhikr *born of the will*
only paves the road to hell.

To receive *dhikr* in the second manner, from a perfect master, is like having the seed planted in fertile soil. Under the care and nurturing of a perfect master, the seed of *dhikr* planted in the heart will take root, grow and bear fruit.

Dhikr handed down by a perfect master can be divided into two types: 'vocal *dhikr*' (*dhikr-i jalī*) and '*dhikr* of the heart' (*dhikr-i khafī*). *Dhikr-i jalī* refers to *dhikr* that is said vocally and generally in a loud voice. This *dhikr* takes place in sufi gatherings or in the sufi *khānaqāh*. In this instance, the sufis gather together in a circle and chant the 'vocal *dhikr*' harmoniously under the direction of the master or shaikh of the *ṭarīqat*. *Dhikr-i jalī* is regularly practiced by such sufi orders as the Qādirī. Other orders, however, prefer '*dhikr* of the heart'.

In the beginning, it is recommended that disciples pay attention to the utterance of the Name, while at the same time attempting to attend to the significance of the Name. The utterance of the Name is necessary for awakening the heart since the heart of the beginner is more easily awakened by the utterance than by the meaning. Thus, in the early stages of the path, the master encourages 'vocal *dhikr*'. However, as the heart gradually becomes familiar with that which is being remembered, it ceases to need 'vocal *dhikr*'. Although *dhikr-i jalī* is sometimes practiced in the presence of the shaikh during gatherings of the Nimatullahi Sufi Order, it is *dhikr-i khafī* that is stressed.

Dhikr-i khafī or *qalbī* (also 'of the heart') is *dhikr* integrated with the rhythm of breathing such that not a single breath passes without the remembrance of God. With *dhikr-i khafī*, there is no need for a special gathering; moreover, no vocal utterance is necessary.

Some masters have described *dhikr* as a spiritual wine, saying that *dhikr-i jalī* is like spilling the wine down your shirtfront, while *dhikr-i khafī* is like drinking down the wine and getting drunk.

> *There is no grace for the heart and soul*
> *in the* dhikr *of the tongue.*
> *Spiritual wine will not rob you of reason*
> *if you pour it down your shirt.*

Many verses of the Koran and Traditions of the Prophet refer to *dhikr-i khafī*:

> Remember your Lord in your heart, humbly with awe and without utterance, at dawn and at dark, and be not amongst the neglectful. (7:205)

The hearts of those who believe are set at rest by God's remembrance; indeed, by God's remembrance (only) are hearts set at rest. (13:28)

Be patient with those who call unto their Lord, morning and evening, seeking His pleasure. Indeed, do not turn your eyes from them, as if you were attracted merely to the veneer of the life of the world. Do not follow the one whose heart We have turned away from Our remembrance and who follows his own desires and wanders from his purpose. (18:28)

The highest remembrance is *dhikr-i khafī*. (Saying of the Prophet, cited by Rūzbihān in *Mashrab al-arwāḥ*)

Said God, the most Mighty and Precious, 'For one who remembers Me inwardly, I remember him outwardly.' (Imām Ḥusayn, cited by Kulaynī in *Uṣūl-i Kāfī*)

Said God, the most Mighty and Precious, 'I take form in the thoughts of My worshippers, and I am with them when they remember Me. If they remember Me inwardly, I will remember them inwardly, and if they remember Me outwardly, I will remember them outwardly, for My remembrance is the greater . . .' (a Tradition cited by Shāh Ni'matullāh in the first book of the *Rasā'il*).

One who remembers God, the most Mighty and Precious, inwardly, truly remembers Him over and over. Verily, they were hypocrites who remembered God outwardly, but not inwardly. The Koran says, ". . . They deceived the people and remembered God but little" (Imam 'Alī, cited by Kulaynī in *Uṣūl-i Kāfī*).

When God says, 'Remember your Lord in your heart, humbly and with awe,' even the angel who records it knows not the merit of that remembrance in a person's heart, for it is so great that only God can know it. (*Uṣūl-i Kāfī*)

O Lord, busy our hearts with remembrance of You above all other remembrances and occupy our tongues with thanks to You above all other thankfulness. O Lord, open my heart to Your loving-kindness, and fill me with Your Remembrance. (Imām Zayn al-'Ābidīn, *Ṣaḥīfa-yi Sajjādīya*)

The Rules and Manners of *Dhikr*

When performing *dhikr*, one should follow certain practices:

1. The disciple should at all times be purified by ablution (*wuḍū*).[1]

2. One should wear clean clothes.

3. One should have a pleasant smell.

4. One should sit facing the *qibla* (the direction of Islamic prayer, toward Mecca).

5. It is recommended that one sit with eyes closed.

6. In the course of *dhikr*, one should appeal internally for the master's help.

7. The disciple should sit on the knees with the legs folded under, placing the palm of the right hand on the left thigh and grasping the right wrist with the left hand. In this manner, the legs and arms both form the word '*lā*', which in Arabic means 'no' or 'not'. This position stresses the sufi's nothingness and the negation of the sense of 'I-ness'. Thus, the body is in harmony with the inner state, which is the negation of the 'self'.

8. One should empty one's heart of everything but God, forgetting even the very self, focusing attention completely on God. For example, one omits the vocative particle, '*Yā'* ('O' in English) in invoking God's Name. Thus, instead of saying "*Yā Ḥaqq*" ('O God'), one says just, "*Ḥaqq*". The sufi in the state of *dhikr* is not aware of himself or herself as a separate entity who could call upon another. One who is aware of self in the state of *dhikr* is no better than a liar.

9. Disciples should try to remain silent, speaking no more than is necessary.

10. Disciples practicing *dhikr* should not object to whatever condition descends upon them, whether spiritual contraction or expansion, sickness or health, pleasure or pain. They accept all conditions equally and are content, never turning away from God.

How *Dhikr* Takes Effect

Remembering the Divine is not the occupation
of any useless idler,
and returning to God is not the way
of any worthless wanderer.

—Rūmī

Three conditions are necessary for *dhikr* to have its effect:

1. The seed of *dhikr* must be nourished by the loving-kindness (*maḥabba*) that issues through the master.
2. The terrain of the sufi's heart must be furrowed by the plow of devotion.
3. The plant that grows from the seed must be tended by the master until it bears the fruit of loving-kindness in the disciple.

The *dhikr* that has been inculcated by a master who is in the true 'chain of succession of masters' is the fruit of the tree of loving-kindness. Such a *dhikr* is like a fertile seed ready to be sown. If the *dhikr* comes from a master not in this succession, however, it is like a defective seed which, though planted in the disciple's heart, has little chance of growing. Moreover, even if it should grow, it would be vulnerable to pestilence and disease.

The seed of loving-kindness that is planted in the sufi's heart is nurtured and protected from pestilence through the attention of the master, for the true master has traveled the path and seen the dangers that threaten the traveler. He or she knows how to deal with each situation in which the seed of loving-kindness and devotion is endangered, and is able to foster it so that it may grow safely to maturity and bear fruit. *Dhikr* is the spiritual connection between master and disciple. By means of this connection to the master, the disciple, from the earliest stages, becomes linked to God. Thus, the disciple who lacks devotion to the master cannot benefit from the *dhikr* that the master has bestowed.

On the other hand, a master who lacks a link with the Divine and is not the manifestation of God's Perfection will merely lead the disciple into egotism and self-worship rather than devotion to God.

The Results and Fruit of *Dhikr*

While the distractions of the senses can be overcome through observance of the *sharī'at*, the distractions of the self (*nafs*) which darken and agitate the heart can be averted only by the devoted practice of *dhikr*—a practice based upon the negation of the thought of everything but God. When the light of *dhikr* clears the heart of the darkness of agitation, the heart becomes aroused and gradually steals the *dhikr* from the tongue, making *dhikr* its preoccupation.

Dhikr rends all the veils that are woven by the self's desires and attachments. As the darkness of the heart is lessened, these veils are removed and the light of *dhikr* shines fully upon the heart. At the same time, however, anxiety is also created in the heart. This anxiety is not fear; it is the dread of losing this new-found state and returning to the previous one. It is an anxiety mixed with eagerness, enthusiasm and hope. In reference to this, the Koran states, "Verily, the believers are those upon whose hearts fear descends when God's Name is remembered" (8:2).

By the water of *dhikr*, the harshness and aggressiveness in the heart become washed away and are replaced with smoothness and softness. By the light of *dhikr*, the darkness that frightens and threatens the heart is dissipated and dispelled. As is written in the Koran, "Then their skins and their hearts become gentle with the remembrance of God" (39:23).

The continuous practice of *dhikr* causes the 'Lord of *dhikr*' to dominate the kingdom of the heart, driving away whatever is not the thought of Him. Once the 'Lord of *dhikr*' has taken up residence, the heart grows attached and finds peace, to the extent that whatever is not Him will now be turned away. As the Koran states, "The hearts of those who believe are set at rest through God's remembrance; indeed by God's remembrance (only) are hearts set at rest" (13:28). In the words of Shaikh Majd al-Dīn Baghdādī:

Inasmuch as the heart
is touched by the ways of the world,
so will the hand be stayed
from mastering the ways of the world.
Once there was a heart
and a thousand different thoughts;
Now there is naught
but Lā ilāha ill Allāh.

The sufi text, *Mirṣād al-'Ibād*, describes the above process in this manner:

> The king of love sends down to the city of the heart the royal banner which is planted at the crossroads where the heart and spirit and body and soul meet. He has the royal constable of yearning capture and bind the wayward self with the rope of seeking, bringing it to the execution place of the heart. There, at the base of the royal banner of love, its head of desire is severed by the sword of *dhikr* and hung upon the tree of devotion.

As Rūmī has written in the *Mathnawī*:

The howl of monsters has a familiar ring,
'Tis a call to oblivion that they sing.

They cry, "Come hither! We'll give you a name."
They cajole the caravan, proffering fame.

The monsters tempt man with artful seduction,
Leading him on to final destruction.

It is just at the end that these monsters take shape
As the ravenous wolf and lion at the gate.

The monsters cry out, "Reputation!"
"Fatten your purse and cherish high station!"

Boring subtly within, they slyly insist;
Yet the secrets are opened to those who resist.
Remembrance of God can these voices banish;
In the inner eye's light will these vultures vanish.

Remembrance of a thing brings its qualities to existence,
As every accident needs an essence for subsistence.

In *Mirṣād al-'Ibād*, the negative qualities dominating the self are symbolized as hoodlums and thugs, who, after surrendering and becoming slaves, respond in the words of the repentant Adam and Eve, "O Our Lord, we have wronged ourselves; if Thou forgive us not and have not mercy on us, we will surely be among the lost" (Koran, 7:23). According to the text, the king of love absolves the delinquents of their misdoings and bestows the cloak of bondage upon them, raising them to the rank of chamberlains of the heart.

Only when the realm of the heart has been purified of the agitation of the self's negative qualities and the mirror of the heart polished of its rust does the heart deserve to be raised to the kingdom of the beauty of Unity and freedom from need.

In the Prophet's words, knock at a door,
and it will finally be opened to you.
Wait on the street of a friend,
and you will finally see his face.
Dig all day in the earth,
and eventually you will reach pure water.

—Rūmī

At this point, the king of love accedes to the throne of the heart and the minister of reason stands at the gate. The city of the heart becomes resplendent with the radiance of certainty and devotion, sincerity and generosity, trust in God and all the noblest virtues. The real King now arrives at the hidden chamber of the heart and the original Beloved reveals her true Beauty.

But love is jealous and will not rest until even these noble courtiers, in their turn, are driven forth from the throne of the heart by force of *Lā ilāha* ("There is no god. . ."), for even these positive qualities represent a vestige of 'otherness' to be rejected.

Once this occurs, the heart has reached the truth that is rightfully its own, recovering its pre-eternal purity and becoming the castle of the royal *ill Allāh* (" . . but God"). The King has emptied the heart of any 'otherness' and made it His own realm, as described in the Koranic passage, "And all faces shall be humbled before the everlasting and self-subsistent God" (20:11). This is the state referred to in the Sacred Tradition, "Neither My earth nor My heaven can encompass Me, yet the heart of My adorer contains Me." From this point on, the command of God dominates all the attributes and parts of the Perfected One in accordance with the Koranic passage, "And truly, God is predominate over His affairs" (12:21). In other words, no attribute or part can dominate by its own will unless God so wills and commands. This is the meaning of the Sacred Tradition:

I become his ear, so he can listen with that ear.
I become his eye, so he can see with that eye.
I become his tongue, so he can speak with that tongue.

I become his hand, so he can grasp with that hand.
And I become his foot, so he can walk with that foot.

Here, the heart has finally become the abode for the manifestation of all God's Attributes.

The Different Names of God and the Greatest Name

Some of the Names of God identify the Divine Essence, while others indicate the Divine Attributes. It is up to the master to decide which of these to inculcate, according to the disciple's capacity and spiritual state. It should be understood, though, that whenever one of the Divine Names is remembered, God is being remembered by all of His Names at once. As Shāh Ni'matullāh has said:

For all of God's names the essence is One.
So all of the names are in fact but One.

It should also be understood that the Greatest Name of God is actually like a kind of alchemy or '*Sīmurgh*'.[2] In the words of Ja'far Ṣādiq, "Free your heart from all that is not the remembrance of God. Then call Him by whatever name you wish, and that becomes the Greatest Name."

The Repetition of *Dhikr*

Some shaikhs of the path have prescribed a specific number of repetitions of each *dhikr*. For example, the Name 'Allāh' might be repeated sixty-six times because that is the sum of its letters when valued according to one numerological system.

Other shaikhs, however, have not considered the number of repetitions to be important. This is, in fact, correct since attention to the number of repetitions will only destroy the concentration and state of the sufi. Moreover, how can one forget the self—one of the conditions of *dhikr*—while attending to the process of enumeration? In the words of Bāyazīd, "*Dhikr* is measured not in number, but in intensity of presence."

The Stages of *Dhikr*

There are various stages of *dhikr*.

1. *Dhikr* is remembered with the tongue, but not felt in the heart. Some shaikhs have said that even when *dhikr* is experienced only verbally, it has at least some effect.

2. The heart, as well as the tongue, becomes involved in remembrance, but *dhikr* has not yet become firmly established in the heart. Here, one should make an effort to pretend that *dhikr* has taken root so that the heart will continue to be aroused by it. Without the presence of such continued effort, the heart will go its own way and turn away from remembrance.

3. *Dhikr* comes to dominate the heart and becomes firmly rooted. Now, only great effort can detach the heart from its remembrance and involve it in the remembrance of anything else.

4. That which is remembered (God), rather than the remembrance, comes to dominate the heart. At this point, there is no question as to whether the *dhikr* should be in Arabic or Persian or English, for the words of the *dhikr* are the concern only of the *nafs* (self). Here, the traveler, in complete involvement with the Beloved, forgets even the Name of God. This is the first step of Sufism and the beginning of 'passing away of the self in God' (*fanā'*) in which both the sufi and the remembrance have been forgotten! The sufi in this state says:

So lost did I become from myself
through Your remembrance on the path,
that now I ask for news about myself
from anyone I pass.

Sanā'ī, in *Ḥadīqat al-ḥaqīqa*, has written:

Striving on the path is but remembrance of God,
not hanging idly around the gatherings of the path.

Though remembrance is your guide at first,
you'll get to the point where even it becomes a burden.

The diver seeking for a way in the depths of the ocean
is killed in the end by that same deep ocean.

The dove being absent from God says, 'coo, coo'[3]
if 'you' is still present, how can you shout 'Hū'?[4]

Those in God's presence are content facing calamity;
if you're not in God's presence, give vent to your shrieks.

The stages of *dhikr* have also been described in the following manner:

1. *Dhikr* of the ordinary ones—the profit of which is to take the traveler away from negligence.
2. *Dhikr* of the elect—the tearing away of the veil of reason and discernment from the rememberer, with the whole heart becoming attentive to God.
3. *Dhikr* of the elect of the elect—the passing away of the rememberer in the One who is remembered.

Many other statements have been made about the stages of *dhikr*. According to Shāh Ni'matullāh, while in the beginning the rememberers think they are remembering God, at the end they realize that it is actually God who is remembering God and thus there is no longer any perception of *dhikr*, for God is now both rememberer and remembrance.

Bāyazīd has described his experience thus, "Thirty years I spent in remembrance of God. When I stopped, I realized that my very *dhikr* was my veil." Junayd has stated, "Sufism is at first a remembrance, then an ecstasy, then neither one nor the other, until finally nothing remains as it truly never had been."

In the words of Abu'l-Ḥasan Nūrī, "The truth of *dhikr* is the passing away of the *dhākir* (rememberer) in the *madhkūr* (One who is remembered)."

'Aṭṭār, in *Tadhkirat al-awliyā'*, has recounted the following incident from the life of Junayd:

> It is said that on one occasion a disciple violated the ethics of Junayd's order and therefore left the service of the master. He set out on a journey, traveling until he came upon another group of sufis. One day Junayd passed by and saw him, whereupon the devotee was overcome with awe at the master's presence and fell down, cutting his head so that it bled profusely. Each drop of blood flowed in such a way as to form the Name 'Allāh'. Junayd, upon seeing this,

> reproached the devotee for making the claim that he had reached the state to which his remembrance aspired, saying that any child could come this far and that only a true man might reach the Remembered.

Rūmī, in his account of the love of Zulaykhā for Joseph, has written:

When Zulaykhā sought to call out
Joseph's name,
'incense', 'rue' and 'aloes'
all meant the same.

Within these names, his true name
did she hide,
which only to intimates
she did confide.

If a hundred thousand names she gathered
in a heap,
she meant just 'Joseph', which in her heart
she did keep.

In hunger, she would quote his name
and be lifted up.
Thirsty, she would drink and swoon
with nectar from that cup.

Joseph's name in ecstasy would quench
her fervid thirst,
for by that heavenly mead
was her state of rapture nursed.

If from his name
she should one moment feel pain,
At that moment, from this pain,
benefit she would gain.

Transcendent warmth against the cold,
like a fleecy cover,
by love's name glowed
upon the yearning lover.

Water round the fish gives
it its daily bread,
one element at once food and drink,
dress and bed.

So is the lover like a babe
drinking milk from the breast,
knowing naught on the way
but that over-flowing blessedness.

Dhikr is the product of God's loving-kindness (*maḥabba*), the seed being the loving-kindness implanted in the sufi's heart by God and the fruit being the sufi's remembrance of God. As the Koran says, "He loves them, and they love Him" (5:54). That is, God's loving-kindness always precedes humanity's. Until God loves a devotee and remembers that one, it will be difficult for the devotee to remember and love God.

Dhikr also awakens intuition in the heart, enabling it to perceive the Divine Attributes and inspiring the traveler to love God. This familiarity with God brings about a lasting peace in the sufi's heart. "Indeed, by God's remembrance are hearts set at rest" (Koran, 13:28).

The truth of *dhikr*, then, is that it is God who first remembers the disciple. Thus, some sufi mystics have interpreted the Koranic passage, "Verily, prayer restrains one from evil, and certainly the remembrance of God is greatest" (29:45), to mean that while daily prayer is a remembrance performed by order of Islam to restrain one from misdoing, the greater remembrance is God's remembrance of humanity. In the same way, the inculcation of *dhikr* by the master of the path is considered a kind of 'greater remembrance'. In the words of the sufi mystic Rūzbihān:

> *Dhikr* is a light emanating from God's manifestation. By its purity, the hearts of sufis are drawn to the Beloved.

1 *wuḍū*: the ritual washing performed before saying daily prayers (*namāz*) in Islam.

2 See 'Aṭṭār's *Conference of the Birds*.

3 '*coo*': in Persian, a way of saying, "Where is he?"

4 *Hū*: one of the Names of God in Arabic, meaning 'He'.

Contemplation

O brother, you are your very thought.
As for the rest, you are only hair and bone.
If your thought is a rose, you're a garden of roses.
But if it's a thorn, you're just fuel for the stove.

—Rūmī

Fikr is defined in the dictionary as contemplation or reflection. The Koran has many passages referring to *fikr.*

> ...Verily in this matter there are signs for those who reflect. (This phrase comes at the end of many verses.)
>
> We sent down to you this scripture that you might clarify to the people whatever descends upon them so that they might reflect. (16:44)
>
> There are those who remember God standing and sitting and reclining, and who reflect upon the creation of heaven and earth. (3:190)
>
> Thus, God makes clear to you His signs that you might reflect (upon them). (2:266)

> Thus, We explain fully the signs for those who reflect. (10:24)
>
> So tell them parables that they might reflect. (7:176)
>
> And We sent forth proverbs to the people that they might reflect (upon them). (59:21)
>
> And We sent amongst you love and compassion. Verily, in this there are signs for those who reflect. (30:21)
>
> Say, 'Are the blind and the seeing alike? Should you not then reflect?' (6:50)

A number of Prophetic Traditions also speak about the practice of *fikr*:

> An hour's reflection is worth more than seventy years of worship.
>
> Reflection causes the enlightenment of the heart.
>
> There is no worship like reflection.
>
> And in the words of 'Alī, "Awaken your heart with reflection."

Contemplation from the Viewpoint of the *'Ārif*

An *'ārif* is one who strives to reach God by means of knowledge and virtue. Whereas a philosopher draws two premises together with the intellect in order to generate a conclusion, the *'ārif* draws two kinds of knowledge together in the heart in order to reach a third and different kind of knowledge. For the *'ārif*, this is the significance of contemplation. As long as this third kind of knowledge is not acquired, the *'ārif* considers himself or herself to be involved only in recollection of previous knowledge.

According to Ghazālī in *Kīmīyā-yi Sa'ādat*, contemplation brings about a succession of developments: first, an awareness (*ma'rifat*), then a quality (*ḥālat*), and finally an action (*'amal*).

Contemplation from the Viewpoint of the Sufi

For sufis, the object of contemplation is the Absolute Beloved, everything else being purged from the mind. Whereas the contemplation of the *'ārif* is done primarily with the intellect, the contemplation of the sufi is done more with the heart and is more involved with love. That is, the contemplation of the *'ārif* and that of the sufi are not the same.

In describing these two kinds of contemplation, it is useful to consider the following definitions that various *'ārifs* and sufi shaikhs, according to their different spiritual states, have given:

1. The noblest and most worthy gathering is to sit in contemplation in the garden of Unity. (Junayd)

2. Contemplation is the heart's grasping of the meaning of objects for the sake of comprehending the Subject. (Jurjānī)

3. Contemplation is to be effaced in the remembrance of God. (Shāh Muḥammad Darābī)

4. The one who prays and fasts is near to people, while the one who contemplates is near to God. (Shaikh Abu'l-Ḥasan Kharaqānī)

5. Whosoever contemplates properly can neither speak nor act without sincerity. (Abū 'Amra Najīd)

6. Sitting in contemplation for one hour in the state of witnessing is worth more than a thousand accepted pilgrimages. ('Aṭṭār)

7. Speech without wisdom is a plague, and silence without contemplation is lust and negligence, and the noblest action is to contemplate with self-negation. (Ḥasan Baṣrī)

8. Contemplation penetrates manifestations so as to perceive the work of the Divine. (Ḥārith Muḥāsibī)

9. One hour in contemplation is worth more than a night of prayer. (Ḥasan Baṣrī)

10. The apostles asked Jesus if there was anyone like him on earth. 'Yes,' he replied, 'anyone whose speech is invocation, whose silence is contemplation, and whose perception is opened by awareness of the signs'. (Ghazālī)

11. Thought for the ordinary person is plunging into the sea of illusion, while contemplation for the elect is being immersed in the ocean of understanding. (Rūzbihān)

12. Contemplation brings you to God, while prayer brings you God's rewards. That which brings you to God has more value than that which brings you to something other than

God. (Fakhr-i Rāzī)

13. In the beginning, contemplation directs one's attention towards the understanding that is needed, while at the end contemplation turns one from knowledge to inquiry, from form to meaning, and from the created to the Creator. (Shāh Ni'matullāh)

Contemplation as Practiced by the *'Ārif*

The practice of contemplation for the *'ārif* is carried out in two stages, upon the self and upon God.

1. Contemplation upon the Self

Contemplation upon the self is referred to in the Koranic passage in which God says, "Do they not reflect upon themselves?" (30:8).

In this kind of contemplation, the *'ārif* undertakes a process of analyzing his or her weaknesses and negative qualities, both outward and inward, while at the same time striving to isolate and purge them. The *'ārif* also assesses his or her positive qualities and attempts to cultivate them so that they ornament one's being. Ḥasan, the saint of Baṣra and disciple of 'Alī, taught that contemplation is a mirror that reflects a person's good and bad qualities.

For *'ārif*s, contemplation upon the self may also involve pondering from where and how they have come into existence, for what purpose they exist, and where they are going. Here, they reflect upon the Koranic passage, "Verily, it is from God we come and it is to God we shall return" (2:156), and know that they have come from God and will return to God. Thus, they consider how they can go towards God and what they can do to please God. They might also concentrate upon the meaning of the Sacred Tradition, "I was a hidden Treasure. I desired to be known; thus I created the world that it might know Me."

Day and night my only thought
is why I am ignorant of the states of my heart.
From whence have I come and why?
Where am I headed? Will You not show me my home?

How rapturous the day I fly towards the Friend's abode,
beating my wings in hope of reaching that home.

—Rūmī

Still another object of contemplation for *'ārif*s may be the fact that everything other than the Truth is null and void, and that whatever is null and void cannot know the Truth. Similarly, they may reflect upon the fact that they are a part and God the Whole, and that the part can never comprehend the Whole. Here, the *'ārif* attempts to relinquish all that is null and void in order to arrive at the Truth, endeavoring to leave the part and merge with the Whole so as to perceive in all parts the Whole through Its eye.

Reflection is passing from the false to the True,
transcending the part to perceive the Whole.

—Shabistarī

In regard to contemplation upon the self, *'ārif*s have said, "Your contemplation upon yourself is sufficient for you (to know God)."

2. Contemplation upon God

There are three kinds of contemplation upon God: contemplation upon the Essence, contemplation upon the Attributes, and contemplation upon the Effects.

Contemplation upon the Essence

Contemplation upon the Essence of God is impossible since the temporary cannot reflect upon the Eternal nor the illusory comprehend the Real. In the words of Shāh Ni'matullāh:

Since whatever is not God is null and void,
how can such nothingness ever reach the Eternal?

Ghazālī, in *Kīmīyā-yi Sa'ādat,* recounts that ibn 'Abbās, cousin and companion of the Prophet, once told Muḥammad that some people were attempting to reflect upon the Essence of God. The Prophet replied that they should reflect instead upon the creations of God rather than upon God

Himself, "For indeed," he added, "you do not have the capacity to reflect upon the Essence." As Sanā'ī has said:

The intellect can as easily reach
God's deepest Essence
as a piece of floating wreckage can reach
the depths of the ocean.

Muḥammad has said, "Reflect upon everything except the Essence of God." And Imām Riḍā advised, "Whatever conception you have of a thing, conceive of God as independent of it."

The Prophet recommended that we refrain from making
the Essence of God the subject of our reflection.

Though you think contemplating His Essence is possible,
in fact your view with the Essence has no connection.

Since on the way to God thousands of veils exist,
to think you contemplate His Essence is only imagination.

—Rūmī

Contemplation upon the Attributes

Since the Attributes of God are the same as His Essence, contemplation upon the truth of them is as difficult as contemplation upon the Essence itself. However, it is possible to traverse the Divine Attributes in the sense that the traveler, through continuous remembrance of the various Names of the Attributes, exposes himself or herself to the Grace inherent in them. The individual will therefore absorb this Grace according to his or her capacity and potential. From some Names, the traveler may even be so filled with them that he or she becomes, to some extent, the manifestation of the Attributes. That is, in accordance with the statement, "You become qualified with the Qualities of God," the traveler here may reach the state (*ḥāl*) of 'having passed away in the Divine Attributes'.

Contemplation upon the Effects

The effects of God can be witnessed, and therefore contemplated, both within the self and outside the self. In both instances, one is led from the effect to the Cause, from the creation to the Creator, and from the realm of the defined (limited existence) to the Undefined or Unbounded (Absolute Existence). Contemplation upon the effects of God, however, will have results only if one is liberated from the desires of the self, for those who are entangled in the demands of the self suffer from a kind of illness and therefore contemplate in an unbalanced way. Imām Muḥammad Bāqir advised his followers not to reflect upon the Essence of God, but rather to reflect upon the grandeur of the creation if they sought to contemplate God's Greatness. In the words of Shaikh Shabistarī:

Though contemplation on God's gifts is a requirement,
contemplation upon the Essence is only a transgression.

Contemplation upon the Essence is useless and vain, for
it's impossible to acquire what's already been gained.

Since all that exists is illuminated by God's Essence,
that which exists cannot illuminate the Essence.

As all the universe is by His light manifested, how can
He be comprehended by that which is manifested?

The light of the Essence cannot be contained by the signs,
for the light of His Glory is triumphant over the signs.

When Junayd was asked about contemplation, he replied that it had several aspects. Contemplation upon the Divine signs, he explained, leads to knowledge of God. Contemplation upon the Divine gifts brings about loving-kindness. Contemplation upon the attributes of the self and God's mercy towards the self produces shame in the individual. And contemplation upon the Divine admonishments, and punishments and rewards, results in fear of God.

Junayd added that if someone questions why contemplation upon the Divine admonishments produces fear of God, it should be explained that those who become involved in such contemplation will conclude that they are going to be punished for past sins and, therefore, will give up their trust in God's generosity, leading them to commit further sins. By committing more and more sins, they will eventually be led to the fear of God. (cited in 'Aṭṭār's *Tadhkirat al-awlīyā'*)

At this point, it may be useful to consider contemplation as described by Khwāja 'Abdullāh Anṣārī. In his book, *Ṣad Maydān* (*A Hundred Fields of Battle*), Anṣārī has taught that contemplation grows out of the sphere of control (where the desires of the self are resisted). According to Anṣārī, the heart travels the path just as the self does, and contemplation for the heart is the impetus for such traveling.

Anṣārī has defined contemplation in the *Ṣad Maydān* as a process of putting together known data in order to arrive at the Unknown. He proceeds to divide contemplation into three categories—the prohibited contemplation, the recommended contemplation, and the necessary contemplation.

> 1. There are three types of prohibited contemplation: contemplation upon the Divine Essence, which is the seed of bewilderment (since the Essence cannot be comprehended); contemplation upon the Divine rewards and punishments, which is the seed of reviling (since one will be unable to accept God's ways); and contemplation upon the secrets of creation, which is the seed of hostility (since one will be unable to decipher these secrets).
>
> 2. There are also three types of recommended contemplation: contemplation upon the creations of the Creator, which is the seed of wisdom; contemplation upon the variety of creation, which is the seed of insight; and contemplation upon God's gifts, which is the seed of loving-kindness.
>
> 3. The necessary contemplation, which is of primary importance, is upon one's own tasks. This consists of analyzing one's shortcomings in obedience to God, which is the seed of shame. Contemplation here also involves reflecting upon one's duties and responsibilities in the future, this contemplation being the seed of fear.

Included in the necessary contemplation is the cultivation of a sense of 'spiritual supplication' (*niyāz*), the merit of which is to see God. Cultivating such a sense of supplication involves contemplation, reflection and retrospection. The contemplation is upon deeds (how one should act), the reflection is upon discourse (what one should say), and the retrospection is upon forgiveness (how one should forgive). From such contemplation, one understands that one's deeds should be virtuous, one's discourse true, and one's forgiveness pure.

In another book, *Manāzil al-Sā'irīn*, Anṣārī has taught that contemplation is the seeking of insight so as to be able to better comprehend the Sought-for. In this instance, he has also divided contemplation into three categories:

> 1. Contemplation upon the Truth of the Divine Unity, which is merging with the ocean of self-negation and refutation (i.e. the state in which everything is God and there is no longer any 'I' and 'you'). Liberation from this ocean of self-negation is impossible, Anṣārī has stated, except by the light of discovery and appeal to knowledge.
>
> 2. Contemplation upon the subtle intricacies of the creation, which is the water that slakes the thirst of wisdom.
>
> 3. Contemplation upon the meaning of one's actions and states, which makes traveling on the path easier.

Anṣārī has elaborated upon these three types of contemplation by stating that release from the first can occur through knowledge of the limitations of reason, discouragement in attaining the Unattainable End, and grasping the rope of the exaltation of God. The subtle intricacies of the creation, which are the object of the second type of contemplation, can be comprehended by acceptance with contentment of whatever God brings, receptiveness to the Divine Will, and liberation from the bonds of desire.

The third kind of contemplation, upon the meaning of one's actions and states, can be accomplished by the pursuit of knowledge, detachment from social customs, and awareness of those moments when one is involved in what is not God.

Contemplation in Sufi Practice

Contemplation for the sufi is the traversing of the path in the heart, born through the remembrance of God. By the remembrance of God, the lightning of Divine manifestations comes to illuminate the house of the heart. With this illumination, the heart's contemplation becomes awakened and is transformed into a guide on the path of truth.

While 'rational' contemplation is woven, 'heart-based' contemplation is to be found. In rational contemplation, the motivation and guiding force is reason, whereas in heart-based contemplation the motivation and master is God alone.

Give up your reason and be with the One,
for a bat cannot bear the light of the sun.

Wherever the light of God is the guide,
what need is there for Gabriel's advice?

—Shabistarī

Three kinds of heart-based contemplation can be enumerated:

1. Contemplation in the State of Seeking

For the person who is in a state of seeking but has not yet found a master and begun to travel the spiritual path (*ṭarīqat*), contemplation begins when God creates in his or her heart the thought of finding a spiritual guide. By means of this contemplation, a state of restlessness is created in the seeker that does not cease until he or she has found what has been lost. This can occur, however, only if such a one receives the grace of partaking from the banquet of love.

Contemplation should occur in such a fashion
as to open the path and bring forth a king.
Consider that one a king who is free from his kingship
though his radiance lights up the moon and the sun.

—Rūmī

2. Contemplation for the Initiate

For the beginner on the spiritual path, one whose languid thought has not yet been kindled by the warmth of remembrance, contemplation is the revelation in the heart of the master's spiritual beauty by means of illumination. Hence, some masters of the path have said that contemplation is the manifestation of the spiritual face of the master.

3. Contemplation for the Advanced Sufi

From the warmth of remembrance, the languid thought of the sufi is gradually stirred to life and the spirit (*ruḥ*) grows familiar with the Hidden. Some sufi mystics have said that contemplation is the journeying of the heart through the spheres of the Hidden. According to Dhuʾl-Nūn of Egypt, "He who contemplates with the heart has the Hidden revealed to the spirit."

Thus, contemplation for the advanced sufi results from

remembrance and thereby becomes a guide on the path. In the words of 'Aṭṭār:

> *Contemplation is the traveler's guide on the path,*
> *a guide acquired through constant remembrance.*
>
> *Remembrance is what brings forth contemplation, which*
> *in turn brings forth a thousand hidden meanings.*
>
> *Rational contemplation is fine for discourse, but*
> *the heart's contemplation is for the one of action.*
>
> *Though contemplation be for only an hour,*
> *still it's better than seventy years of prayer.*

Or in the words of Rūmī:

> *So much we've said, you reflect upon the rest;*
> *if that doesn't work, then turn to* dhikr.
>
> *Remembrance is what arouses the heart's contemplation,*
> *so make it a sun for your languid reflection.*
>
> *Though the principle of the matter is divine attraction,*
> *O sufi, don't depend upon that and neglect your duties.*
>
> *Since relinquishing such duties is only arrogance,*
> *how can you compare it to losing your existence?*

Concerning this true contemplation, Shaikh Abu'l-Ḥasan Kharaqānī has said:

> God bestowed upon me a contemplation such that I perceived in it everything He has created. I became totally immersed in this contemplation. It became my preoccupation night and day until it opened the eye of my heart and turned into harshness, loving-kindness, fear and heaviness. From that contemplation, I became plunged into Divine Unity and reached the point where contemplation was transformed into wisdom, guidance upon the direct path, and kindness for the whole of creation. I could find no one kinder than myself among all of His creation. I wished to die instead of all of the creation so that death would never be encountered again. I wished Him to judge me

> instead of all the creation so that no one would be judged on the Day of Judgment. And I wished to reap all of the retribution meted out to humanity so that no one would ever have to experience hell.

About this same kind of contemplation, Rūmī has written:

Your thought is only the form;
His thought is the spirit within it.
Your currency is only paper,
but His has gold behind it.

And in the words of Ḥāfiẓ :

Thought and opinion have no place
in the world of the true sufis,
For to be self-centered and opinionated
is a sure transgression on our way.
In the circle of destiny,
we are but a dot made by the compass:
Your contemplation is our grace,
and Your command our only reference.

Meditation

I was drawn to the Beloved
like a moth to the flame;
When I came to my senses,
I was burned up in His fire.

—'Āshiq-i Iṣfahānī

Murāqiba is two people taking care of and protecting each other. The sages of the path have said about *murāqiba* that just as God takes care of and protects humanity, so too human beings in their hearts must take care of and protect their relationship with God. Ibn 'Arabī has written:

> *Meditate upon God in all situations,*
> *for God meditates upon you.*

As it is said in the Koran, "Verily, God watches over you" (4:1) and "God watches over all things" (33:52).

The Meaning of Meditation for the Sufi

Murāqiba is keeping oneself away from what is not God, both outwardly and inwardly, and concentrating one's whole being upon God. Sufi masters have given many definitions of *murāqiba*, among them:

> *Murāqiba* is being inwardly pure towards God, both when alone and with people. (Ibrāhīm al-Khawwāṣ)
>
> *Murāqiba* is relinquishing the control and will of the self, followed by the expectation of God's Grace and Will, and turning away from whatever is not God. (Kashshāf, *Iṣṭilāḥāt-i funūn*)
>
> *Murāqiba* is the presence of the heart with God and the absence of the heart from all that is other than God. (*Ghiyās al -lughāt*)
>
> *Murāqiba* is the protection of one's being from all that is not Divine and the concentration of one's attention upon God. (the *Iṣṭilāḥāt* of 'Abd al-Razzāq-i Kāshānī)
>
> *Murāqiba* is the observance of the secrets with regard to God. (*Asrār al-fātiḥa*)

In the words of Rūzbihān, "*Murāqiba* is the involvement of the spirit (*ruḥ*) in God's Breath." This statement refers to the Prophetic Tradition that declares, "Verily, the Lord has provided Breath for all your days; put yourself in its way" (*Iḥyā al-'ulūm*). Rūmī has written:

The Prophet said, "The Divine Breath
these days is coming forth;
so keep your inner ear aware
and steal this Breath away."

Among you came a Breath, then it passed,
bestowing on whomever it wished a soul.
Another Breath will soon come forth:
O sufi, keep watchful, or you'll miss this too.

The Kinds of Meditation

Murāqiba is in two directions: from God to the creation, and from the creation to God.

1. From God to the Creation

The Divine Meditation towards the Whole of Creation

The world of substances exists only insofar as it is sustained through accidents. Whenever an accident through which a substance subsists fades away, that substance will also cease to subsist. Since each accident will finally cease to exist at one time or another, God must continually watch over the heavenly and earthly substances so that when one particular accident perishes, a similar or contrasting accident is created by Him, thus preserving the existence of those substances. This is the true meaning of the Koranic passage, "At every moment He is involved with creation" (55:29). Rūzbihān has said:

> *Murāqiba* is God's awareness over every particle of the creation from the Divine Throne to the lowest phenomenon, and His overseeing of all the Attributes for the purpose of granting them grace.

The Divine Meditation that Evokes Religious Action

By God's attention upon them, His devotees are stirred to perform the actions sanctioned by Islam and to refrain from those that are prohibited.

The Divine Meditation Towards the Elect

Here, God pays attention to His friends in order to see what they will do for Him. This *murāqiba* is described in the Koranic passage, "Verily, God has purchased from the faithful their selves and their goods" (9:111).

> *God is my customer; He takes me up,*
> *for only He can purchase me.*
>
> —Rūmī

The *murāqiba* of the elect is known only to God, for according to a Sacred Tradition, "My saints are under my shelter; no one knows them but Me." These friends of God are satisfied and made content from this *murāqiba*, as described in the Koranic verse, "Be aware, the friends of God have no fear and no sorrow" (10:62).

2. From the Creation to God

The Meditation of Islam

The *murāqiba* of Islam is the result of attention to God's utterance, "Does he not know that God sees him?" (96:14). In this *murāqiba*, human beings know that God is aware of what they do. Thus, they are watchful for God watches them. Khwāja 'Abdullāh Anṣārī has told the following story in this regard:

> Ibn 'Umar happened upon a slave taking a flock of sheep to pasture. He said, "O slave, sell me one of these sheep." The slave replied that the sheep did not belong to him. Ibn 'Umar then said, "If the owner asks, tell him that a wolf has eaten it." The slave asked, "Where then is God?" Ibn 'Umar was so pleased with this reply that he bought the slave and sheep from the owner and set the man free, giving him the sheep for his own.

Those who practice this kind of *murāqiba* should be watchful over both their thoughts and their actions. In *Kīmīyā-yi Sa'ādat*, Ghazālī has written:

> In the *murāqiba* of thought, one should make an effort to maintain those thoughts that are from God and to relinquish those that are from the self. In the *murāqiba* of action, one should be watchful over all of one's conduct whether that conduct is obedient, sinful, or neither one nor the other. That is, with obedient conduct, one should endeavor to act with devotion and presence of heart. With sinful acts, one should feel shame and strive to refrain from such acts. And with actions that are neither sinful nor obedient, one should attempt always to be polite and to see the Giver in divine gifts, knowing that one is always in God's presence.

Khwāja 'Abdullāh Anṣārī has called this *murāqiba* of Islam the "*murāqiba* of service" and said that it is the result of three things:

1. Obedience to the Divine commands.
2. Knowledge of the prescribed behavior and customs.
3. Awareness of one's hypocrisy.

In the words of Rūmī:

Each moment you'll see the results of your work
if you're watchful and manage to stay alert.

If you've grasped the rope of being vigilant,
your yearning won't have to last to the Judgment Day.
Be watchful if you want to achieve a heart,
for after each action something will be acquired.
If your striving is even greater than this,
you'll rise yet higher than murāqiba.

The Meditation of Faith

The *murāqiba* of faith is the result of being surrendered to God, as described in the Koranic passage, "Soon We will show them Our signs in the world and in their selves" (41:53). A person involved in such *murāqiba* observes God's signs both in the outside world and in the world of selves, and moreover sees God as the doer in everything.

A man once asked Ibn Mubārak to advise him. The answer he received was, "Watch for God." The man then asked for the interpretation of this statement and was told, "Always be in a state as if you were seeing God." Anṣārī has called this *murāqiba*, the "*murāqiba* of time," and said that it can be attained through three things:

1. Annihilation of all desires.
2. Purification of all thoughts.
3. Predominance of kindness.

The Divine Meditation

The Divine *murāqiba* is reserved for the saints of God, who see Him both inwardly and outwardly, in both solitude and society, and who say, "I see nothing unless I have seen God first."

Anṣārī has called this meditation, the "*murāqiba* of the secrets," stating that it too can be reached through three things:

1. Being lost to the world.
2. Abandoning the self.
3. Being filled with closeness to God.

This meditation has also been called the *murāqiba* of the sincere ones. The hearts of such beings are drowned in God, and their attention never strays to anything other than God. Sometimes, they are so drowned in God that if you talk to them they don't hear, and if you stand before them they don't see.

'Abdullāh ibn Zayd was once asked if he knew anyone who was truly absorbed in the Creator rather than the creation. In answer, he addressed 'Ibāt al-Ghulām, who had just arrived. "Who did you see on the way coming here?" 'Ibāt al-Ghulām replied, "No one." Ibn Zayd then pointed that the man's way had been through the crowded bazaar.

To summarize then, there are two kinds of meditation for sufis: the outward *murāqiba* and the inward *murāqiba.*

The outward *murāqiba* involves the attention of the part (i.e. the individual) towards the Whole (i.e. God). Sufis in this state see God in everything. Whatever they do is for God, and whatever befalls them, they know to have come from God.

The inward *murāqiba* involves the attention of the Whole towards the Whole. Here, the sufi closes the eye that sees only fragments of Reality and opens the vision of the total Reality, in which the Divine meditates upon the Divine. This is the ultimate *murāqiba* for sufis, the only true meditation.

The Conditions of Meditation

The place where meditation occurs should:

1. Be empty of everything other than God (that is, it should be a secluded place).

2. Be on the ground floor of a building preferably so that the arrival and departure of others won't cause one to turn away from the state of meditation.

3. Be quiet.

4. Be clean.

5. Be soft and comfortable so that one's attention won't be distracted from God to oneself. (In the past, sufi masters have used sheepskins for this purpose.)

6. Be free of any kind of odor so that one's sense of smell will not distract one.

The Rules and Manners of Meditation

In meditation, the sufi should:

1. Have performed ablution (*wuḍū*).

2. Wear soft and light clothes, with buttons undone so as to keep the body completely comfortable.

3. Sit on the floor or ground.

4. Keep the body free from motion. (Shiblī once saw Nūrī meditating in such a state of stillness that even the hair of his body was motionless. He asked Nūrī from whom he had learned such meditation. Nūrī replied, "From a cat I saw sitting at a mouse hole. In waiting for the mouse, the cat was even more still than I am now.")

5. Keep the eyes shut.

6. Close the window of thought and imagination, and forget everything but God, especially when starting to meditate.

7. Concentrate upon God and witnessing the writing on the heart. (In this, it is necessary to be instructed orally by the master or shaikh.)

8. Lose any sense of individual will to the extent of forgetting even one's identity as the one meditating.

9. Abandon all desires. (In the state of mediation, various desires, wishes and fantasies will appear in one's memory and thought, causing one to be distracted from the direct path. Therefore, these obstacles must be demolished. To accomplish this, there are special orders that have been handed down by the masters of the path which must be received orally from the master or shaikh.)

10. Face the *qibla*, the direction of Islamic prayer. (Although it is certainly correct as stated in the Koran that "...wherever you turn, you find the face of God" (2:1150), by facing the *qibla* the meditator's outward attention is directed towards the outer Ka'ba, the house of God in Mecca, and thus is in harmony with his or her inward attention, which should be directed towards

the inner Ka'ba, namely, the heart or Throne of God.)

11. Develop the habit of meditating at least fifteen minutes in each 24-hour cycle, preferably during the hours of darkness.

The Positions of Meditation

The sufi may choose among three positions in meditation:

> 1. Sitting erect on the knees with the legs folded under, placing the palm of the right hand on the left thigh and grasping the right wrist with the left hand (Fig. 1). In this manner, the legs together form the Arabic word *lā,* which means 'no' or 'not'. The arms also form the same word. As previously stated in the chapter on *dhikr,* this position stresses the sufi's nothingness and the negation of the sense of 'I-ness'.
>
> 2. Sitting in the same position as figure one, except with the legs crossed. Here, both the arms and legs form the word '*lā*' (Fig. 2).
>
> 3. Sitting cross-legged, with knees raised and arms folded around the legs, with the left hand grasping the right wrist and head bowed slightly towards the heart. (Fig. 3). In this position, the same '*lā*' shape is formed. In the past, sufis often tied a *rishta* (a belt made of threads loosely tied together at intervals) around the legs in order to maintain this position for a long period of time without tiring.

For extended periods of meditation the sufi may sit in the same position as figure three and rest the head, at the left eyebrow, on the left knee. Sa'dī, in the *Gulistān,* tells the story of a sufi who, while meditating in this position, became totally drowned in the ocean of discovery. When the sufi returned from this state, a companion asked him what gift he had brought back to his brethren from the garden. The sufi replied, "I had in my mind that when I reached a rosebush, I would fill up the skirt of my robe with roses. But when I finally approached the rosebush, I became so drunk with the aroma of the roses that I lost my hold on my garment."

In the case of physical disability, the sufi may also sit on a chair with legs bent and parallel, head held upright, and hands in the same position as figure one.

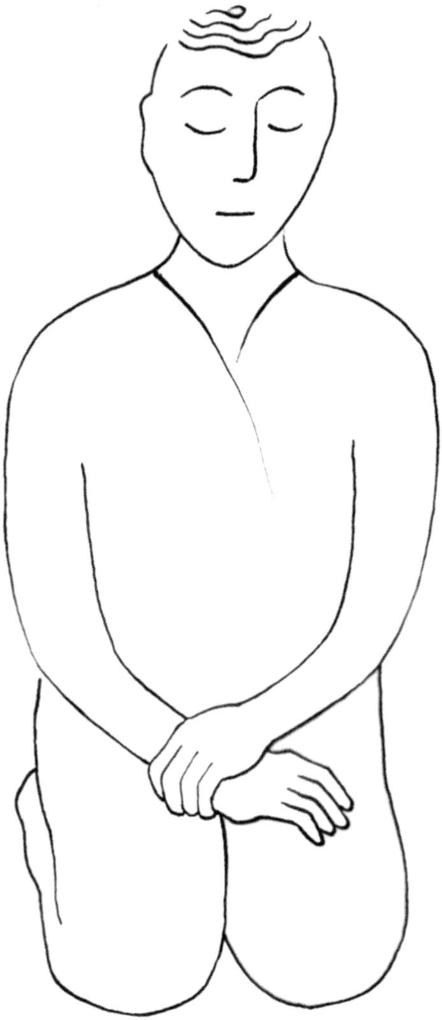

Figure 1

Figure 2

Figure 3

The Benefit of Meditation for the Initiate

In the early stages of the path, meditation provides a way of practicing self-control. After a great deal of effort, it leads to the point where one's restless thought becomes restrained and one's heart attains calmness and serenity, accompanied by closeness to God. Certainly, for one who lacks self-control, meditation will initially be difficult. But gradually, through the attention and assistance of the master, this difficulty will be dissolved.

For the beginner then, the result of success in meditation will be the development of self-control, leading to the attainment of a 'unity of attention' to God.

The Benefit of Meditation for Advanced Sufis

Meditation is one of the basic conditions for the attainment of voluntary death, which is the aim of the *ṭarīqat* or spiritual path. When the sufi arrives at peace-of-heart and closeness to God, such a person becomes the possessor of the *nafs-i muṭma'inah* ('self at rest'). To the Divine Call, "O Self at Rest," the sufi now replies by involvement in the meditation of "...return to your Lord, well-pleased [with God], [and] God well-pleased with thee" (Koran, 89:28). Shāh Ni'matullāh has said in this regard:

> Sufis in this state (*ḥāl*) concentrate upon the Divine Gifts for the sake of receiving the gracious Breaths of Absolute Being. They turn away from whatever is not God and become drowned like us in the ocean of loving-kindness. They long to see the Beloved, as foretold in the Sacred Traditions, "Know you that the yearning of the saints to see Me is long" and "Verily, My longing for them is still stronger." Their hearts and spirits, rather than their flesh and blood, hasten day and night to be in the Divine Presence, and their spirits long to receive eternal life from the Beloved.

As a result of such meditation, sufis gradually become estranged from the world of 'I' and 'you'. They eventually lose even the sense of meditation with its lingering quality of duality as God causes them to die to themselves and brings them to life in Himself.

Self-Examination

We cannot pick dates from the thistles we grew,
and we cannot get silk from the wool we wove.
We drew no line of contrition through
our sins in the ledger,
And inscribed no merits beside
our capital transgressions.

—Sa'dī

As defined in the dictionary, *muḥāsiba* means to balance accounts or to be precise in calculating. In sufi terminology, *muḥāsiba*, or self-examination, means to take account of one's actions and thoughts in traveling towards God, to know that God always keeps a record of what one does.The Koran has many passages indicating that God keeps account of one's actions:

> And verily, whether you manifest what is within you or keep it hidden, God will call you to account for it. (2:284)

> Be aware! His is the Judgment, and He is the swiftest Reckoner. (6:62)

> Their Lord metes out their reward, for God is swift in reckoning. (3:198)

> Be in awe of God; verily, God is swift in reckoning. (5:4)
>
> They receive retribution to the extent that they deserve, for God is a swift Reckoner. (14:51)
>
> For the disbelievers, their actions resemble mirages on the plain; in their thirst they reckon that they are reaching water, yet they find nothing but God and His Reckoning; and God is a swift Reckoner. (24:39)
>
> Verily, it is for you to inform and for Us to call to account. (13:40)

The following Koranic passage explicitly describes *muḥāsiba*:

> O you who believe, be aware of God and look well into yourselves to see what you have in stock for tomorrow. (59:18)

And in the words of the Prophet of Islam:

> Take account of your actions, before God takes account of you, and weigh yourself before you are weighed, and die before you die (cited in the *Ḥadīth* collection, *Al-minh aj al-qāwī*).

Sayings of the Greatest Sufis About Self-Examination

1. Abū 'Uthmān Maghribī has said, "The noblest action on this path is the examination of the self and the performance of one's duties with knowledge." (cited by 'Aṭṭār in *Tadhkirat al-awliyā'*)

2. Ghazālī, in *Kīmīyā'-i Sa'ādat*, has written:

> Just before going to sleep each night, the devotee should take account of what the *nafs* (self) has done during that day, so that one's profits and losses get separated from one's investments. The investments here are the necessary actions; the profits are the recommended actions; and the losses are those actions that have been prohibited.
>
> Just as one would purchase with care from a wily merchant, so one must bargain with caution in dealing with the self, for the self is a tricky and deceitful impostor that has a way of presenting its purposes in the garb of spiritual obedience so that one considers as profit what was really loss. In fact, with every action that is questionable, the devotee should examine his or her motivation carefully. If it

> is determined that the motivation came from the self, then compensation should be demanded of it.

3. In *Ṣad Maydān*, Anṣārī has written:

> The eleventh field of battle is *muḥāsiba*. It develops out of the field of purification and has three foundations:
>
> > Eliminating vicious deeds from one's dealings.
> >
> > Balancing Divine gifts with devoted service.
> >
> > Separating one's portion (i.e. that which is achieved through striving) from His portion (i.e. that which is bestowed by God).
>
> The way of achieving the first foundation is to know that all actions in which the self is involved are vicious and destructive.
>
> The way of achieving the second foundation is to know that one's unawareness of receiving Divine gifts is due solely to one's shortcomings and that for all the Divine gifts of which one is aware but ungrateful, compensation must be given. It is also to know that the misuse of Divine gifts will lead only to the destruction of one's belief.
>
> Achieving the third foundation involves knowing that service performed to gain something in this world is one's own concern, that service performed to gain something in the hereafter is one's obligation, while service performed to reach God is one's price (i.e. God determines one's spiritual worth by the degree of one's service to Him).

4. In *Mashrab al-arwāḥ*, Rūzbihān has stated that *muḥāsiba* is the intellect's enumeration of one's inner transgressions and one's thoughts of what is not God, along with its blaming of the 'commanding self' (*nafs-i 'ammārah*) for following its own desires. In this station of attending to religion, the intellect is a protector of the spirit (*ruḥ*).

Rūzbihān goes on to quote one mystic as saying that *muḥāsiba* is striving unceasingly to discipline the self so as to transform it. The mystic adds that once the station of *muḥāsiba* is reached, *murāqiba* (meditation) becomes purified and the beauty of the *ādāb* (rules and manners) of being in solitude and performing devotional observances becomes illuminated. According to this mystic, the essence of *muḥāsiba* is that the angelic forces of the universe present to the spirit (*ruḥ*) the transgressions that have been committed by the self (*nafs*).

5. Suhrawardī, in describing the process by which a particular state (*ḥāl*) is sometimes transformed into a station (*maqām*), has also spoken of *muḥāsiba*. In *'Awārif al-ma'ārif*, he has explained that while the motivation for *muḥāsiba* is originally awakened in the inner being of the devotee, this motivation fades as the attributes of the self reassert their dominance. It then returns, only to fade once again.

In other words, due to the manifestation of the attributes of the self, the devotee's state keeps vacillating until he or she finally receives Divine assistance and the state of *muḥāsiba* becomes dominant. Here, the self is subdued and *muḥāsiba* takes over the devotee's freewill. *Muḥāsiba* is now one's sole abode, having become a station rather than a state. Thus, the state of *muḥāsiba* is transformed into the station of *muḥāsiba*.

Once the devotee resides in the station of *muḥāsiba*, the state of *murāqiba* becomes awakened. This state also rises and fades in one, however, as negligence and error from time to time arise in one's inner being. Only when such negligence and error are dispelled through Divine assistance does *murāqiba* itself become a station.

In the first instance, the station of *muḥāsiba* does not become firmly settled in the devotee until the state of *murāqiba* begins to descend upon him or her. Similarly, the station of *murāqiba* does not become firmly settled in the devotee until the state of *mushāhada* (witnessing) begins to manifest. When this state of witnessing occurs, then *murāqiba* becomes a station.

6. Muḥammad Ibn Maḥmūd Āmuli, in *Nafāyis al-funūn*, has written:

> *Muḥāsiba* means constantly searching into and examining the states and actions of the self. Day by day and hour by hour, one should take account of whatever arises in one's being, whether positive or negative, so as to become aware of the qualities of one's states.

Āmulī adds that *muḥāsiba* is regarded as the third of the traveler's stations on the path.

In the early period of Islam, there existed a sufi order known as the Muḥāsibiya, which was founded by Ḥārith Muḥāsibī (b. Baṣra 781, d. Baghdad 857 A.D.), a contemporary of Aḥmad Ibn Ḥanbal (the founder of the Ḥanbali school of Islamic Law). In *Tadhkirat al-awlīyā'*, 'Aṭṭār has written that Ḥārith was given the title of Muḥāsibī because of his rigorous and assiduous devotion to the practice of *muḥāsiba*. According to 'Aṭṭār, Ḥārith has said:

Those who truly practice *muḥāsiba* possess certain characteristics that become manifested in their speech and action. Through God's grace, such people reach the higher stations of the path by means of their practice of *muḥāsiba.* This can take place, however, only by having a strong will and rejecting the desires of the self. For one who acquires a strong will, opposition to the desires of the self will be easy. Thus, it is essential to develop one's will and to nurture the following characteristics that are known to bear fruit:

Never swearing in the Name of God, whether accidentally or deliberately, rightly or wrongly.

Never lying.

Never breaking a promise if at all feasible, while avoiding making promises as much as possible.

Never cursing another person (asking God to bring calamity upon that person), even one who has done harm.

Never intending ill towards other people (whether in word or deed) or praying for them to be punished, but rather tolerating everyone and everything for the sake of God.

Never accusing another person of infidelity, polytheism (*shirk*), or the causing of discord—for accusing anyone of such acts leads the traveler farther from having grace upon people and closer to the Divine Wrath.

Never having the intention to commit sins, either outwardly or inwardly (that is, dissociating one's whole being from everything other than God).

Never putting the burden of one's pain or suffering on anyone else's shoulders, whether or not one's personal need is involved.

Never having any greed whatsoever or envying the possessions of others.

Never considering oneself higher than anyone else—for in this way one will arrive at nearness to God both in this world and the hereafter, thereby attaining a truly high spiritual station and the perfection of honor.

The Kinds of Self-Examination

Muḥāsiba-yi nafsī (of the self)

Each night before sleeping, sufis should take a few minutes to examine their selves and enumerate all the positive and negative actions they have done during the day. If they find that their negative acts have outnumbered their positive ones, they should resolve to compensate for this imbalance the following day. If their positive acts have been more numerous, they should not only avoid any sense of pride, but resolve to redouble their efforts at eliminating all negative acts the next day. In the event that their positive and negative acts are balanced, they should endeavor to add to their positive ones.

Sufis should also take account of their thoughts in this kind of *muḥāsiba*. They should weigh their positive and negative thoughts carefully, gradually emptying their minds of the negative ones and replacing them with positive ones, for God calls sufis to answer even for their negative thoughts. Junayd has told the following story in this regard:

> I was once sitting outside the Shuniziya Mosque in Baghdad waiting for a funeral ceremony to take place. All the people of Baghdad were there to pray for the dead man. Among them, I saw a poor man begging with a pious look. I thought to myself, "If only this beggar worked in order to provide for himself, it would be better."
>
> When I returned home that evening and went about my customary observances, I found it difficult to perform my prayers and invocations. Because of this unaccustomed difficulty, I was forced to remain awake until late at night. Suddenly, I fell asleep. In a dream I saw the beggar being brought to me at a banquet table and I was told to eat of his flesh since I had gossiped behind his back.[1]
>
> I replied that I had not gossiped behind his back, but only thought something to myself. The answer I received was, "You are not like ordinary people. From you even such thoughts cannot be accepted, and therefore you must ask for forgiveness from this man."
>
> The next morning I searched for the man but couldn't find him anywhere. Finally, I came upon him by a stream where chives were being washed. He was sitting at the edge of the stream catching the stray greens which slipped through the washers' fingers and floated downstream.
>
> I greeted him and went to speak, but he interrupted me, saying, "O Abu'l Qāsim, are you going to

think such thoughts again?" I told him no, and he replied, "May God forgive us both." (cited in *Tarjuma-yi Risālā-yi Qushayriyya*)

Muḥāsiba-yi ṭariqatī (of the path)

The condition of the '*muḥāsiba* of the path' is that sufis take account of their states, striving as much as possible to decrease their states of multiplicity and increase their states of Unity. In this way, they will advance each day towards the Divine Reality, coming ever closer to God. Here, one should remember the Tradition of the Prophet which states, "That one whose days are equal is one who has lost."

Sufis climb a ladder at the top of which is God. They should not count the rungs they have climbed, but rather take account of the way they have yet to travel.

Sufis should always be cognizant of the contracts they have with God and of their commitments to the master, refraining from breaking these promises. They should be aware of the constant presence of the master and strive never to make any move contrary of the orders of the path.

With each step that sufis make, they should take account of God, knowing that all their movements are for the sake of God. Just as every breath they take is in remembrance of God, every movement they make is for the sake of God.

Finally, having surrendered themselves completely to God, sufis should consider whatever comes to them as being descended from the Divine and, therefore, good.

Muḥāsiba-yi Ḥaqqī (of the Divine)

Shaikhs of the path should adapt their outer and inner being to the different kinds of states and stations that they have. For example, when in the state of being in contact with others, they should be careful not to fall into self-worship. When in the station of being in contact with the Creator, they should refrain from speaking of their existence.

The claims of shaikhs should always be appropriate to their situations. Moreover, whatever they claim to be, they should in fact be. In this kind of *muḥāsiba*, shaikhs should take account of their responsibilities not only to God on the one hand but to their disciples on the other. In the station of Unity, they should not speak of 'I' and 'you' or of their spiritual discoveries and abilities. In the realm of purification and loving-kindness, they should never be harsh or severe. And in the station of guiding, they should be careful not to become a veil between the disciple and God.

One who claims to be a 'master of the path' should step upon both this world and the hereafter rather than be greedy for the wealth of the world. The Perfected One is a stranger to whatever is not God and not the acquaintance of the possessors of wealth or rank. In the words of Shāh Ni'matullāh:

> *Muḥāsiba,* at the beginning, is a balancing of accounts between negative and positive acts. At the end, it is the actualization of pure Unity—in both the station of 'Unity in multiplicity' (being inwardly absorbed in God, while outwardly existing in the world) and 'Unity in Unity' (being outwardly and inwardly absorbed in God).

[1] A reference to the Koranic verse which says, "O you who believe, refrain from being too free in your suspicions, for some suspicions are sinful, and do not meddle in other people's affairs or gossip about others. Would any of you care to eat the flesh of his dead brother? Surely you would not; fear God then. Verily, God is forgiving (to the repentant) and the Most Merciful" (49:12).

Initiation

Do not enter the 'Tavern of Ruin'
without observing its manners,
for the dwellers at its door
are the confidants of the King.

—Ḥāfiẓ

Entering the path of the people of the heart involves observing certain 'rules and manners' (*ādāb*) and ceremonies which for centuries have been respected and adhered to by sufis. These 'rules and manners' and ceremonies have been handed down and followed by the masters of the path up to the present time.

In view of the command, "Travel the path in the way that others have traveled it before," these rules and manners have been enumerated herein and their secrets and meanings explained so that this work may be a guide for seekers.

The Five *Ghusls*[1]

Before being initiated into the world of spiritual poverty (*faqr*), those who seek to travel towards God must first perform *niyyat*[2] and then five *ghusls* in the manner described below:

Ghusl of Repentance (*tawba*)

With this *ghusl*, the seeker repents from his or her former misdoings and strayings. He or she also apologizes, when becoming joined to the worship of God, for the previous sin of self-worship.

Ghusl of Submission (*Islam*)

In the *ghusl* of submission, the seeker who is not already a Muslim makes a vow (*niyyat*) to accept Islam and become a Muslim. If one is already a Muslim by tongue or tradition, one vows to become committed with heart and spirit (*ruḥ*) to Islam and to behave in agreement with its principles.

In accordance with the saying of 'Alī, "Islam is surrendering," the seeker should become surrendered fully to God's Will, both outwardly and inwardly, and be content with whatever God desires.

Ghusl of Initiation into Spiritual Poverty (*faqr*)

To enter into the world of spiritual poverty, one must be pure both outwardly and inwardly. Thus, one performs a *ghusl* outwardly and cleanses the outer being so that the inner being will also incline towards purity:

Purify thyself: then proceed to the 'Tavern of Ruin'
that it not be polluted by you.

—Ḥāfiẓ

Ghusl of Pilgrimage (*ziyārat*)

It is a tradition when visiting people deserving of respect in the world to cleanse one's body and put on clean clothes. Similarly, when making a pilgrimage to the Perfected One, or master of the path (*pīr-i ṭarīqat)*, one should be cleansed and purified in the same manner.

First become purified, and then
Look upon that Pure One.

—Ḥāfiẓ

For this reason, the seeker performs a *ghusl* cleansing the outer being and puts on clean clothes before approaching the master to acquire the orders of the path.

Ghusl of Fulfillment (*qaḍā-yi Hājat*)

Since the 'supplication' (*niyāz*) of the seeker in traveling along the path is to reach the rank of the Perfected One, a *ghusl* for the fulfillment of this aim is performed before coming into the master's presence.

The Five Symbols of Spiritual Poverty

After the seeker has performed the five *ghusls*, he or she prepares five objects that are taken into the master's presence and given to the master so that the seeker on the path of the travelers toward Unity may be accepted and guided. These five objects are: a few yards of white cloth, a whole nutmeg, a ring, a coin, and some rock candy. Each of these objects is symbolic of a certain commitment made by the one who seeks to travel towards God. These commitments are represented by objects so that they will remain fixed in the traveler's mind and never be forgotten.

White Cloth (*chilwar*)

The white cloth taken into the master's presence represents the traveler's shroud and indicates that the traveler, like a dead body in the hands of a *ghassāl* (one who washes the dead), has become surrendered fully to God. In doing so, he or she considers the master's orders as God's orders and obeys them without ever questioning 'how' or 'why'.

Whole Nutmeg (*juz*)

Juz represents the head of the traveler. In presenting *juz* to the master, the traveler consents to never reveal the Divine secrets that are confided in him or her. That is, even if threatened with decapitation, one should not reveal such secrets. In other words, the traveler's head is symbolically presented to the master here as a hostage for God's secrets.

Ring (*angushtar*)

The ring given to the master upon entering the world of spiritual poverty represents the band worn by slaves in olden times and signifies the traveler's devotion to God. In presenting this ring to the master, the traveler vows to become devoted solely to God and to give up the desire for anything else.

Coin (*sikka*)

The coin symbolizes the wealth and riches of the world. The traveler, in presenting this coin to the master, promises to empty the heart of any desire for the wealth of the world. Here, it should be noted, the object is to have no *attachment* to wealth. If the sufi is rich one day, then poor the next, he or she remains unaffected by either condition. In the state of richness, the sufi should be generous, in the state of poverty, joyful and patient.

Rock Candy (*nabāt*)

Nabāt represents the candy given as an offering at the second birth of the seeker. Whereas the seeker's first birth is from his or her mother, the second birth comes upon entering the domain of spiritual poverty. With this re-birth, the seeker steps into the realm of Spirituality, Truth, and Unification, being born from the mother of nature and multiplicity into the world of love (*'ishq*), loving-kindness (*maḥabba*), and Unity (*tawḥīd*).

In presenting this rock candy, the traveler also comes to realize that the path should be traveled with peace of mind and gladness, not with depression and displeasure.

The Five Commitments

Before entering into the circle of spiritual poverty, the seeker makes five commitments to the master. It is only when the seeker accepts and understands the significance of these commitments that the master comes to guide him or her along the straight path of Unity of the Nimatullahi Sufi Order.

Obedience to Islam

The seeker, upon entering the world of the sufis, makes a commitment to

Islam. If he or she has not already been a Muslim, the two testimonies of Islam (*shahādatayn*) should be uttered here. These are : "I testify that there is no god but God" (*Ashhadu an lā ilāha ill Allāh*) and "I testify that Muḥammad is His Prophet" (*Ashhadu anna Muḥammadan rasūl Allāh*).

Kindness towards God's Creatures

With this commitment, the sufi vows never to bother any of God's creatures and to be kind and friendly towards all of them while traveling the path. Here, the sufi should constantly put into practice the words of Sa'dī's poem which states:

I am joyful and content in the world,
for the world is joyful and content from God.
I am in love with all of creation,
for all of the creation belongs to God.

Preservation of the Secrets of the Path

At the beginning of traveling the path (*sulūk*), the sufi makes a commitment not to reveal to anyone the secrets he or she receives—regardless of whether that person is a stranger, friend or fellow darvish. These secrets consist of the remembrance and contemplation he or she is given, as well as all discoveries and revelations witnessed in the world of Unity. Such secrets should be spoken of to no one but the master. In this way, the secret will not fall into the hands of one unable to keep it.

That friend from whom the top of the gallows
became honored
was the one accused of revealing the secrets.

—Ḥāfiẓ

Service on the Path

From the beginning to the end of traveling the path, the sufi must undertake to accept and obey with heart and spirit, and without questioning 'how' and 'why', every order and service that is given by the master. The sufi should know that acting carelessly in such service will only cause one to stray from the path of devotion. So effective is such service that it can be said,

"Whatever the sufi finds, he or she has found from service."

Sa'dī presents a beautiful illustration of service in his poem from the *Būstān* about Sultan Maḥmūd and Ayāz, the Sultan's servant. The poem begins with someone criticizing Maḥmūd by saying, "What wonder this is! Ayāz, his favorite, has no beauty. A flower without color, without any smell, how strange then is the nightingale's attraction!" When told of these words, Maḥmūd replies, "Truly my love is for his virtue, and not for his form or face."

Sa'dī then proceeds to recount the story of how in a royal procession a camel laden with jewels and pearls once stumbled and fell, spilling its precious stones. Sultan Maḥmūd, being generous, gave permission for his followers to plunder the jewels and hastily rode away. All of the followers broke rank and rushed to gather the jewels, neglecting the King for this wealth. Only Ayāz ignored the jewels and followed after the King.

When Maḥmūd saw him following, he called out, "O Ayāz, what has thou gained of the plunder?" In reply, Ayāz declared, "I sought no jewels, but followed my King, for how can I occupy myself with your gifts when all I seek is to serve?" Sa'dī then concludes:

O friend, if you come near to the throne,
neglect not the King for his jewels;
For on this path, the saint never asks
anything of God but Him.
So know if you seek but the grace of the Friend,
you're entangled in your prison, not His.

Dīg jūsh

Upon entering the world of spiritual poverty, the sufi declares inwardly, "I have come in order to sacrifice myself for the Friend."

To demonstrate this, just as Abraham by God's command sacrificed a sheep instead of Ishmael, the sufi (with the master's or shaikh's permission) should have a special meal prepared from a sheep in accordance with the *ādāb* and traditions of spiritual poverty and distribute it among the darvishes. The food so prepared is called *dīg jūsh.*

1 *ghusl:* the act of ablution—the washing of one's body in a prescribed manner for the purpose of purification.

2 *niyyat:* a vow or declaration of one's intention to perform a particular devotional act as in, most commonly, *namāz* (or daily prayer).

Rules and Manners

Till the end of eternity, the perfume of love
will never reach the heart
of the one whose face has not touched the dust
of the Tavern's threshold.

—Ḥāfiẓ

The *khānaqāh* is by definition the private quarters and gathering place of the sufis. It is a place where those of spiritual states can assemble, the school of their inner journey toward perfection. The seekers of God come there to polish the mirror of their hearts and remove the rust of attachment. It is the *ka'ba* of lovers. It is the *qibla* of the sincere, the realm of those who possess the secrets, who are in need of nothing. It is the refuge of the vigilant, who have fearlessly rent open their breasts, torn out their hearts and become totally selfless. Therein dwell the faithful, the companions of purity. There one can hear nothing but the beautiful melodies of the Beloved; one can inhale no fragrance but the gentle air of love and fidelity. Its aspirants have sacrificed all belief, have given up their hearts and have readied themselves for the final leap into total self-abandonment. Everyone is a stranger to them but God. They transcend all reason, yet to the devotees of the intellect they appear mad. Those esteemed high there have set aside 'I' and 'we' for the invocation, 'I am God'.

Indeed, love has many wonders that the intellect considers madness. True and sincere aspiration is needed to shatter the chains of the intellect, to follow the order of 'madness' and leave one's 'self' behind. Thus, in coming to the *khānaqāh*, one will reach a state beyond one's perception and realize that the *khānaqāh* is a manifestation of the Throne of God:

From the terrestrial to the celestial domain,
all veils are torn aside
for the one who serves the goblet
that shows the Universe.

—Ḥāfiẓ

This goblet in which the whole world is manifested is the heart of the Perfect Human Being. The sufi in the *khānaqāh* serves the possessor of this heart. Here, the constant remembrance of God is upon all tongues and the name of the Beloved is engraved on all hearts. The love of the Beloved leaves no place for hostility. The lightning of love and loving-kindness radiates throughout the atmosphere of the *khānaqāh* and illuminates all eyes. Here, inner peace and contentment are achieved. One who is silent here is in meditation and contemplation. One who is speaking says naught but the Beloved's name.

This is no Ka'ba for idiots to circle,
Nor a mosque for the impolite to clamor in.
This is a temple of total ruin.
Inside are the drunk, from pre-eternity
to the Judgment Day, gone from themselves.

—Khwāja 'Iṣmat Bukhārā'ī

Observance of the Manners (*Ādāb*)[1] of the *Khānaqāh*

The essence of Sufism is Islam, and the essence of Islam is true sincerity with God. The quintessence of sincerity is surrender, inward serenity and obedience to the Beloved. Sufis are those of moderation, integrity, friendship and good deeds. Their hearts are in constant remembrance of the Beloved, and their tongues are in the service of the Beloved. Awaiting His command, their eyes are fixed upon the path of the Beloved. This blessing can by no means become possible except by observing the rules and manners of the spiritual path (*ṭarīqat*), of which the *ādāb* of the *khānaqāh* is one essential part. As it is sometimes said: "The whole of Sufism is *ādāb*."

Come to the tavern!
Drink the wine!
Go not to the cell-squatters in the monastery
for their deeds are dark.

—Ḥāfiẓ

Advantages of Going to the *Khānaqāh*

There are many advantages for the sufis in going to the *khānaqāh*. These can be divided into secular and spiritual advantages.

Secular Advantages

1. Through talking and associating with the darvishes in the *khānaqāh*, one acquires the manners of sufis, which are the ethics of humanity. This in itself is of great value. It is necessary for each sufi to learn the proper social behavior for interrelating with those of purity (i.e. the sufis); this is dependent upon going to the *khānaqāh*. As a result, at least outwardly one will be able to call oneself a sufi.

2. Material difficulties and worldly involvement can be resolved through close contact with one's fellow darvishes. This service to one another is the essential basis of all community. In addition, the elimination of such difficulties leaves one more free time for resolving spiritual difficulties.

3. Through associating with one's fellow darvishes, a greater intimacy is promoted among all the members of the *khānaqāh*. From the other darvishes, one acquires the proper manners and behavior of sufis, and thus the qualities of perfection.

4. By regularly attending the *khānaqāh*, one is prevented from going to other gatherings that are colored by the attachments of the world of multiplicity. This a great blessing from which many benefits will ensue.

5. The absence of a sufi on the nights of the meetings causes the *pīr-i dalīl*[2]

and other darvishes to seek out the reason for this absence. Thus, they ask after him or her and seek to offer aid and consolation regarding any difficulties he or she may have.

6. Talking to darvishes whose hearts are pure brings comfort to one's heart and mind.

Spiritual Advantages

1. Going to the *khānaqāh* and seeing one's fellow darvishes reminds the spiritual wayfarer (*sālik*) not to neglect the sacred purpose. Thus, one becomes occupied more than ever with the work of the heart, and so maintains a constant vigilance over the neglectful impulses of the worldly self.

2. The attention of the shaikh and elders of the *khānaqāh* upon the seekers helps greatly to stimulate their inward expansion, further their spiritual development, and aid them in attaining their aim and finishing the spiritual path. With experience, the full significance of this will ultimately become clear to the seeker.

3. Observing the spiritual states of one's fellow darvishes (especially those who with great enthusiasm and deep feeling are constantly engaged in carrying out spiritual duties and service) has a profound effect in stimulating and encouraging the aspirant.

4. The proper conditions and atmosphere for the performance of the duties of the sufi are, in every sense, available in the *khānaqāh*. Thus, the sufi is enabled with no impediment whatsoever to maintain a constant state of remembrance of God.

5. The beginner, in the company of sufis, can better remain in a state of remembrance than if he or she were alone. The benefits gained from the gathering of the sufis are considerably greater than those that would result from being in solitude. The reason for this is that in the sufi gathering multiple breaths achieve a unified harmony with one another. Thus, the participants are unanimously attentive to a single aim and the realizations that result are considerably intensified and heightened:

The wing of Gabriel is spread there
where the sufis invoke Hū.[3]
Contrary to their selves, they cry out drunkenly
in remembrance of God.

Those Responsible for the *Khānaqāh* and Their Functions

Around the tavern door,
the wild, the vigilant swarm,
bestowing and withdrawing
the imperial crown.

—Ḥāfiẓ

The shaikh, *pīr-i dalīl* and *dūdi-dār* (tea master) enlighten and give warmth to the *khānaqāh*.

1. The Shaikh

Both the worldly and the spiritual affairs of the *khānaqāh* are under the supervision of the shaikh. All orders of the shaikh are to be obeyed unquestioningly and unconditionally, and the sufis should never object to them.

Qualifications Upon Which the Shaikh is Selected

The shaikh is selected by the *quṭb* (sufi master) from among people with the following qualifications:

1. He or she should have not less than twelve years experience upon the path of spiritual poverty (*faqr*).

2. He or she should possess an intimate understanding of the duties of a master in relation to a disciple and must be effective in applying them. In addition, he or she should be familiar with the mysteries of spiritual poverty and Sufism (*taṣawwuf*) and be aware of the instructions of loving-kindness and the intimations of love.

3. He or she must have previously been given permission to be a *pīr-i dalīl.*

4. He or she must possess the qualities and virtues of human perfection and be of a generous, self-sacrificing and magnanimous disposition.

When a darvish has fulfilled the above conditions and has surmounted the inward trials to which the sufi master subjects him or her, the honorable robe of guidance is bestowed upon him or her, and he or she is permitted to assist and guide seekers.

The Shaikh's Duties in the *Khanāqāh*

Love itself is your Beloved,
and when you attain to it,
it will tell you what to do.

1. The shaikh must pay constant attention and make every effort to secure and safeguard the *khānaqāh*'s welfare and prosperity.

2. Maintenance and replacement of the equipment of the *khānaqāh* is solely the shaikh's responsibility.

3. Accommodation of darvishes for whatever length of time in the *khānaqāh* must be in accordance with the shaikh's permission.

4. All the shaikh's free time should be spent in the *khānaqāh.*

5. The holding of the various gatherings of the sufis (*dhikr, niyāz, and dīg jūsh*), festivals and funeral ceremonies must be conducted only with the shaikh's approval.

6. The admission to the *khānaqāh* of sufis not belonging to the Nimatullahi Sufi Order should be only with the shaikh's sanction and approval.

7. The shaikh must supply an annual report to the master on his or her own activities, on the welfare and general state of the *khānaqāh*, its financial affairs, and any improvements that he or she has made in the *khānaqāh*'s facilities.

8. The shaikh must be present in the *khānaqāh* on Thursday and Sunday

nights before sunset unless he or she has a valid excuse. The shaikh should depart from the *khānaqāh* in the morning (or at night, if he or she does not keep the night vigil) only after everyone else has left.

9. The shaikh should not seek to increase the number of darvishes. Those who come to the *khānaqāh* have been brought by God and those who abandon the *khānaqāh* have been taken by God.

The Shaikh's Duties to the Darvishes

1. The shaikh is affectionate with all the sufis and does not do anything that might antagonize them.

2. He or she is always careful to observe sufi *ādāb* in the presence of other darvishes, for the shaikh is the supreme example of the principles of sufi behavior.

3. The shaikh does not in any way seek material help from darvishes, but rather may make recommendations for their benefit.

4. The shaikh inquires about the spiritual states and experiences of the darvishes, and (while keeping in mind their individual spiritual capacities) encourages them by reminding them of the behavior and discourses of the great sufis of the path.

5. The shaikh acts in such a way with the darvishes that they understand he or she does not consider himself or herself superior to them because of he or she being a shaikh. Rather, the shaikh considers himself or herself to be beneath them as he or she knows a shaikh's eminence lies in service, and not in being a shaikh.

6. With the sufis the shaikh acts selflessly, with compassion and moderation. The shaikh withholds no blessing or grace from them, nor any of his or her sympathy or advice. If, because of the distractions of the world of multiplicity, a languidness or state of spiritual contraction (*qabḍ*) overcomes the darvishes, the shaikh (by means of encouraging advice and spiritually elevating stories) attempts to polish this dust from the mirror of their inner selves. Thus, once again the fire of ardor will be rekindled in their hearts.

7. Never should the acclamation or praise of others, the revelations of the

shaikh's own spiritual life, his or her traversing of the spiritual stations, or the occurrence of a spiritual state make him or her think that thereby he or she has become perfect or 'in union'. The shaikh should not let the seductions of his or her worldly self deceive him or her.

The Shaikh's Duties to the Master (*Quṭb*)

1. The shaikh seeks inwardly and ceaselessly the grace of the *quṭb* in order to better perform his or her inner and outer tasks.

2. Every month, the shaikh prepares and sends to the *quṭb* a report concerning his or her own and the other darvishes' spiritual progress.

2. *Pīr-i-dalīl* (Counselor)

The *pīr-i dalīl* is the assistant and consultant to the shaikh. Traditionally, the function of the *pīr-i dalīl* has been to reprimand, whereas the shaikh's role has been to console. The selection of the *pīr-i dalīl* depends upon the proposal of the shaikh and the permission of the *quṭb*. The following points should be observed in the choosing of a *pīr-i dalīl*:

1. He or she should have had continuous and prolonged experience in Sufism (over twelve years).

2. He or she should have passed through at least three of the spiritual stations of Sufism.

3. He or she should have the ability to discuss adequately and solve difficult points of mysticism and problems of the spiritual path.

4. He or she must have a deep understanding of different temperaments and the conduct proper for each one.

5. The *pīr-i dalīl* should have perfect cognizance of the secrets and rules of Sufism, as he or she must first instruct anyone seeking to be initiated until the shaikh verifies that person's suitability for initiation. In short, the *pīr-i dalīl* should be able to discuss clearly and present (according to each person's respective capacity) the way, method and aim of Sufism.

6. It is better if he or she has served previously as a *dūdi-dār* (tea master).

The Duties of the *Pīr-i-dalīl*

1. The *pīr-i dalīl* should familiarize those who seek to be initiated with the way, method and aim of Sufism.

2. Before anyone's initiation, the *pīr-i dalīl* should instruct that person in the proper behavior to be observed in the sufi gathering and in meetings with the shaikh and other sufis.

3. If darvishes act contrary to the rules of the *khānaqāh*, they are to be reprimanded by the *pīr-i dalīl.* The sufis know that admonishing by the *pīr-i dalīl* is as necessary as consoling by the shaikh. These admonitions (*tanbīh*, literally 'awakening') are to train the darvishes so that they will not form a careless and inattentive attitude.

4. The organization of the sufi gathering is under the *pīr-i dalīl*'s supervision and is his or her responsibility.

5. The *pīr-i dalīl* must be careful that non-darvishes are not admitted to the sufi gathering except with the explicit permission of the shaikh. Should a darvish bring his or her spouse, child, or friend to the *khānaqāh* on a Thursday or Sunday night, the *pīr-i dalīl* must first obtain the shaikh's permission for that person to attend the gathering. If permission is granted, that person may be allowed to enter.

6. The *pīr-i dalīl* is responsible for supervising the affairs of the *dūdi-dār*, the servitors (*ahl-i khidmat*), and the traveling darvishes residing at the *khānaqāh*.

7. If a darvish who comes regularly to the *khānaqāh* on the appointed nights does not attend one night, the next day the *pīr-i dalīl* should inquire how he or she is. The *pīr-i dalīl* also seeks to aid the darvishes in any difficulties that they might have.

8. If darvishes consult him or her concerning some inner problem or worldly entanglement, the *pīr-i dalīl* should sympathetically and with loving-kindness guide them and help them to resolve it.

3. *Dūdi-dār* (Tea Master)

In all the affairs of the *khānaqāh*, the *dūdi-dār* follows the orders of the *pīr-i dalīl*. The selection of the *dūdi-dār* is also the responsibility of the *pīr-i dalīl* (depending upon the permission of the shaikh and the approval of the *quṭb*). A *dūdi-dār* should possess the following qualifications:

1. He or she should not have less than twelve years experience in Sufism.

2. He or she should have passed through at least two of the spiritual stations of Sufism.

3. He or she should be experienced and tried in Sufism so as to have an adequate understanding of the proper ways of behaving with the darvishes.

4. He or she should be inwardly rich and generous, with high aspirations and a forbearing nature.

5. He or she should possess great endurance and patience, being both dignified and firm, smiling, pure-hearted and courteous.

The Duties of the *Dūdi-dār*

1. With the darvishes, the *dūdi-dār* acts with such great kindness and purity that the excellence of this behavior becomes a strong factor in further motivating them to come to the *khānaqāh*.

2. He or she should prevent the consumption of any sort of drugs in the *khānaqāh*.

3. He or she acts kindly toward travelers staying in the *khānaqāh* and sees to their material needs with the utmost respect and consideration.

4. He or she does not make any distinction among the sufis because of their wealth, parentage or social position, seeing everyone in the same light.

5. He or she cheerfully and open-heartedly greets anyone who comes to the *khānaqāh*, whatever their religion or cultural background, and endeavors to make sure that no one ever leaves the *khānaqāh* with disappointment.

6. He or she should with kindness instruct, admonish and advise the young people of the *khānaqāh*.

7. He or she should not be negligent in maintaining the cleanliness and welfare of the *khānaqāh*.

8. If darvishes speak harshly to the *dūdi-dār*, he or she does not become offended or react against them in return. Rather, the *dūdi-dār* should increase his or her affection toward them and humble himself or herself all the more. This itself is the greatest possible punishment for the darvish.

9. Whenever at any time during the day or night a darvish arrives at the *khānaqāh*, the *dūdi-dār* should greet and treat that visitor with the utmost friendliness, courtesy and respect, preferring the guest's comfort to his or her own.

10. If the equipment of the tearoom (*dūdi*) is in some way deficient or lacking, the *dūdi-dār* should not complain. Rather, he or she must be patient as far as he or she is able. If, however, he or she is unable to do so, the *pīr-i dalīl* may be consulted.

4. Darvishes of Service

Those darvishes who possess inner potential, sincerity and good manners are chosen by the *pīr-i dalīl* for service in the sufi gathering. These darvishes are known as the 'servitors' or 'darvishes of service' (*Ahl-i khidmat*). They are of gentle behavior and are eager to be in the service of the *khānaqāh*.

The Duties of Darvishes in Relation to the Darvishes of Service and Vice Versa

1. Darvishes must highly respect and esteem the servitors.

2. Darvishes should not give orders to the servitors, but if they have some business that they are unable to perform themselves, they may politely request the servitors to do it for them.

3. The servitors should perform the duties assigned to them with dedication and devotion.

4. The servitors should not give priority to any darvish because of his or her wealth, parentage or social position. That is to say, during ceremonies and receptions, they should be careful to treat all equally—passing tea, cookies, etc. around to everyone.[5]

5. In their encounters with everyone, the servitors should observe the manners of darvishes, the highest of all human ethics. They should always consider themselves as servants of all people, especially sufis.

6. In the festivals held at the *khānaqāh*, the servitors must show children the same respect they show adults.

The Duties of the Sufis Concerning the *Khānaqāh*

There are certain duties, outlined below, that the darvishes have to the *khānaqāh*:

1. Darvishes should be neat in appearance and in a purified state when entering the *khānaqāh*, always wearing their cleanest clothes. It might even be wise if they put aside special clothes for going to the *khānaqāh*.

2. If at all possible, darvishes should never come to the *khānaqāh* empty-handed, for as they know:

> *Coming empty-handed to the door of friends*
> *is like going wheatless to the mill.*
>
> —Rūmī

3. Darvishes should estimate the needs of the *khānaqāh* when going there and bring whatever can be afforded.

4. Upon entering the *khānaqāh*, darvishes should completely set aside all thoughts of the world and its affairs.

5. Darvishes should be extremely careful in the maintenance and protection of the equipment of the *khānaqāh*.

6. Darvishes should understand that the *khānaqāh* is the real home of the

sufis, and for their own part, should try as far as possible to help preserve the welfare, prosperity and upkeep of its facilities, not waiting to be reminded of their duties.

7. Whenever possible, darvishes should make contributions to the treasury of the *khānaqāh*. They may give them either to the shaikhs or one of the stewards of the *khānaqāh*. Each darvish should decide how much he or she wishes to give; it is totally his or her responsibility. Furthermore, it is not necessary to pay a fixed amount each month.

8. Darvishes should do everything possible to be present in the *khānaqāh* on Sunday and Thursday nights.

9. If at all possible, darvishes should try to come to the *khānaqāh* before sunset and perform their evening prayers there.

10. When darvishes who are fasting enter the *khānaqāh*, they should inform the *pīr-i dalīl* or *dūdi-dār* of their condition before sunset (the time of breaking the fast in Islam.)

11. At all times, darvishes should prefer attending the *khānaqāh* to the superficial gatherings of the world.

12. In the *khānaqāh*, darvishes should concern themselves with nothing but the remembrance of God in their hearts.

13. In the *khānaqāh*, darvishes must not speak, see, or hear (that is to say, they must not manifest the existence of their 'selves') without the permission and order of the shaikh or the *pīr-i dalīl* of the *khānaqāh*.

14. Darvishes must unhesitatingly accept any food that is offered in the *khānaqāh* and know at all times that whatever comes to them is their own portion and fortune. At all times and in all states, darvishes should be thankful and content with whatever God provides.

15. Without the permission of the *pīr-i dalīl*, darvishes should never perform any service for the *khānaqāh* that has not been assigned to them.

16. If anything causes the darvishes displeasure or irritation in the *khānaqāh*, they should accept and understand this to be what is Divinely intended. They

must never become upset by anyone and should instead humble themselves even further.

The Duties of the Sufis Concerning Those in the *Khānaqāh*

The Duties of the Darvishes to the Shaikh of the *Khānaqāh*

1. Darvishes should know that it is absolutely essential for them to respect the shaikh both inwardly and outwardly. The essence of this duty is superbly expressed in a quatrain by one of the disciples of Shāh Ni'matullāh:

Ni'mat'Alī walked with us
on this path and become
a seeker in the way
of Ni'matullāh.

He made himself small and humble,
acting as an obedient son,
till from the grace of the Shaikh's holy breath,
he became Bābā 'Alī.

2. Without permission, a darvish should not speak in the presence of the shaikh.

3. In the presence of the shaikh, darvishes should be fully respectful. For example, they should not sit carelessly or impolitely with outstretched legs.

4. Darvishes should relate to the shaikh in private those of their visions, dreams, or spiritual experiences that they feel are worthy of notice.

5. Darvishes should not object or take exception to any of the shaikh's actions.

6. The darvishes' welfare depends upon obeying all of the shaikh's orders. In doing so darvishes must neither make excuses nor be negligent.

When the master of your love orders wine,
drink, and await the mercy of God.

—Ḥāfiẓ

7. Darvishes must never try to test the shaikh.

The Duties of the Darvishes to the *Pīr-i dalīl*

1. Darvishes should obey the *pīr-i dalīl*'s orders with heart and soul.

2. Darvishes should show respect for the *pīr-i dalīl* in the sufi gathering.

3. By consulting the *pīr-i dalīl*, darvishes may resolve their spiritual difficulties.

4. Darvishes should refer all seekers wishing to be initiated to the *pīr-i dalīl.*

5. One may consult with the *pīr-i dalīl* concerning worldly, financial, or emotional problems, but should not expect any material help from the *pīr-i dalīl* in return.

The Duties of the Darvishes to the Tea Master

1. Darvishes should be as kind as possible to the *dūdi-dār.*

2. Darvishes have no right whatsoever to give orders to the *dūdi-dār.* If there is anything they need, they may politely request it of the *dūdi-dār.*

3. Darvishes must respect the *dūdi-dār,* knowing that he or she is more advanced on the path than themselves.

The Duties of the Darvishes to Fellow Darvishes

1. Darvishes should show respect to those fellow darvishes who were initiated before them. These darvishes should also be seated in a prior position to them in the assembly. Whoever are eldest on the path take precedence, and must be esteemed. One should not oppose or speak roughly to them, laugh loudly, or act in an unseemly manner in their presence. One must neither talk behind their backs, nor allow oneself to

criticize them in any way. 'Alā al-Dawla Simnānī has related the following account:

> A darvish was in the service of one of my friends. Whenever a negative, disdainful, or scornful feeling concerning that friend came into his heart, for a time he lost his place in my heart. Whenever he felt penitent and begged forgiveness from God, that very moment he regained his place in my heart.

That is, darvishes must be aware that with advanced sufis, they should never cut the thread of sincerity and love with the sword of denial and criticism. All hearts are linked, and all sufis are like a single soul. Whenever darvishes lose their place in the heart of one, they lose their place in the hearts of all.

2. Darvishes must never speak angrily or meanly with one another, or accuse one another of behaving improperly. In their interactions, darvishes should consider themselves below the others. One should know that whenever a darvish has a quarrel with another darvish, the Sufism of both is put into doubt and both will be deprived of God's grace.

3. With fellow darvishes, one should have an open heart and be empathetic and loving. Darvishes should be sincere and withhold nothing from one another, placing themselves totally at each other's disposal, until they find faith from the tree of "Truly, all believers are brothers."

4. Darvishes should never be arrogant, conceited, or act as if they are superior to others—especially because of their parentage, social position, education, or wealth. These trivial attachments are of no importance whatsoever in Sufism.

5. Darvishes should not give orders to their fellow darvishes. However, if there is some task which another is better suited to perform, one may kindly request that person to do it. As far as possible, each darvish should do his or her own work—for darvishes should never impose themselves on anyone.

6. Darvishes should never withhold help from a fellow darvish, nor should they make one feel obligated to help them in turn. Each darvish should instead know his or her own duty and carry it out willingly.

7. If a darvish is a man, he is a brother; if a darvish is a woman, she is a sister;

and one has only love and devotion for one's brothers and sisters.

8. Darvishes should never talk about their own inner realizations, revelations, or miraculous experiences with anyone except the shaikh, nor should they be conceited or arrogant with anyone because of these things.

9. Darvishes should not object to the behavior of other darvishes, or wonder about the 'whys' and 'hows' of another's actions. The personal freedom of every darvish must be observed and respected in the *khānaqāh*. One should never interfere in anyone else's business, for each darvish has his or her own way, state, rapture and universe.

Traveling Darvishes in the *Khānaqāh*

When traveling, it is best if darvishes observe the following rules upon entering the *khānaqāh*:

1. It is not proper for traveling darvishes to enter the *khānaqāh* empty-handed. As far as they are able, they should try to bring some gift or offering, even if it is only a green leaf.

2. A traveling darvish may stay up to three days in the *khānaqāh* as a guest. Any stay longer than that depends upon the shaikh's permission.

3. If a traveling darvish arrives at the *khānaqāh* with his or her family or friends who are not darvishes, he or she may bring them into the *khānaqāh* only with the shaikh's permission.

4. If it so happens that traveling darvishes find themselves unable to reach the *khānaqāh* before sunset, it is better that they spend the night away from the *khānaqāh* and go there the next morning.

5. During their stay at the *khānaqāh*, darvishes should not expect help from anyone. All their expenses are entirely their own responsibility. If, however, the *khānaqāh* has special funds set aside for travelers, their needs will be taken care of.

6. Travelers should have a letter of introduction with them, from either the central *khānaqāh* where the *quṭb* resides, or from the shaikh of their native

city. Upon arrival at the *khānaqāh*, they should present this letter to the shaikh, *pīr-i dalīl* or *dūdi-dār* so as to better introduce themselves.

7. Darvishes residing in the *khānaqāh* for any length of time should actively devote themselves to the service of the *khānaqāh*—its prosperity, welfare and cleanliness. Before their departure, they should carefully clean out and organize their room. If they desire to make a contribution to the *khānaqāh*, they should explicitly inform the *pīr-i dalīl* or the shaikh. If the proposal is accepted, then they should present the contribution to him or her.

8. The rules of the *khānaqāh* should be observed by every traveler and any family memebers traveling with him or her.

General Rules Governing a Sufi Gathering

An assembly that is held in the presence of the *quṭb* or shaikh is said to be a sufi gathering (*majlis-i faqr*). It is obvious then that any gathering that the darvishes organize by themselves without the presence or permission of either the *quṭb* or shaikh cannot be called a genuine sufi gathering.

The following rules of behavior should be observed by all darvishes in the sufi gathering:

1. While sitting, full *ādāb* should be observed. It is preferable for darvishes to sit in the kneeling position (with their legs under them), placing the palm of the right hand on the left thigh. The palm of the left hand should grasp the right wrist. It one cannot sit like this, one may sit cross-legged with the hands arranged in the same way described above. Both of these positions serve to emphasize the negation of the sufi's sense of 'I-ness', and manifest the sufi's nothingness. If one finds it impossible to sit in either of these two positions, then one should leave the gathering. (In a gathering where the *quṭb* is not present, the shaikh is allowed to sit in the special position of 'deep contemplation'. This is not permitted, however, for the other darvishes.

2. Darvishes should not lean against anything while sitting.

3. Darvishes must not be attentive to anything in the world, but rather must be totally absorbed in the remembrance of God in the heart:

One can never get enough
of the ecstasy of seeing You,
just as one can never remain sober
in the circle of Your drunkards.

—Majdhūb-i Tabrīzī

4. Darvishes should never speak with one another during the sufi gathering. Without the shaikh's permission, they should not even begin to speak.

5. Darvishes should refrain from smoking.

6. In the gathering, each darvish is seated according to his or her years of experience on the path. Those eldest on the path sit closest to the shaikh. Family, wealth, or social position are to be considered of no importance in this assembly.

Formalities of the Meal

In laying down and removing the *sufri*[6], the following formalities should be observed:

1. The *pīr-i dalīl,* with the permission of the shaikh, orders the laying down of the *sufrih.* The darvishes of service are responsible for this.

2. Taking the *sufri* in their hands, the darvishes of service kiss the ground reverently before the shaikh, and then spread out the *sufri* before him or her.

3. The first thing that is placed on the *sufri* is salt, then bread and then the rest of the meal.

4. When the meal begins, the others should not commence eating until the shaikh has begun.

5. At the commencement of the meal, all the darvishes eat a bit of salt, saying, "*Bismillāh-i-Raḥmān-i-Raḥīm*" ('In the name of God, the Compassionate and Merciful'), and then begin eating.

6. At the conclusion of the meal, the shaikh does not stop eating until

everyone else has completely ceased. When the meal is over, each person again eats a bit of salt. The shaikh must precede everyone in this action, declaring, "*Al-ḥamdu Lillāhi Rabb al -'Ālamīn*" ('All praise is God's, the Lord of all the Worlds'). Then the shaikh offers a prayer.

7. No one should leave the *sufri* until the shaikh's prayer is over.

8. The collecting and spreading out of the *sufri* is the responsibility solely of the darvishes of service. Without permission, no darvish has any right to help them.

9. The *sufri* should be collected in such a manner that the darvishes finish folding it up before the feet of the shaikh. Before taking the *sufri* from the assembly, they should kiss the ground in reverence before the shaikh.

The Stewards of the *Khānaqāh*

The stewards (*nuzzār*) of the *khānaqāh* are elected from those advanced darvishes who have at least twelve years experience in Sufism. The shaikh appoints three, five, or seven stewards of the *khānaqāh*, while keeping in mind the length of their experience in Sufism, their spiritual development and behavior. The number of stewards varies according to local conditions and area.The duties of the stewards of the *khānaqāh* are as follows:

1. The stewards secure the financial needs of the *khānaqāh* from the darvishes who are individually responsible to determine the sums they wish to give.

2. The expenses entailed in holding the Thursday and Sunday night meetings in the *khānaqāh* are under the supervision of the stewards. The procedure to be followed in meeting the necessary expenses depends upon the situation and income of that particular *khānaqāh*. This procedure is determined and dictated by the *pīr-i dalīl.*

3. The stewards prepare and organize the mourning ceremonies and festivals of the *khānaqāh* while supervised by the *pīr-i dalīl.*

4. The stewards take care of the *khānaqāh*'s building, its repairs, and all its daily expenses according to the orders of the *pīr-i dalīl.*

5. The stewards organize the financial accounts of the *khānaqāh* and the upkeep of its facilities.

6. The stewards help out in the building of any new *khānaqāh*s and volunteer their aid to those already built.

General Advice

Sufis should be open and friendly to members of all religions and nations:

> *Like compasses we are: one foot stable in Islam,*
> *the other voyaging through all religions.*
>
> —Sa'dī

The purpose of our reminder here is to stress that *it would be unfortunate for a lover to turn his or her thoughts to anything other than the Beloved.*

[1] *Ādāb* is a term containing many meanings. Depending on the context it may be translated as 'rules of behavior', 'etiquette', 'rules and manners of social conduct' or a code for sufis. Ādāb has been translated as 'rules and manners' throughout this book.

[2] *Pīr-i dalīl:* counselor, advisor and mediator between the disciple and the master or shaikh.

[3] *Hū*: one of the names of God in Arabic, meaning 'He'.

[4] The nights of the sufi gathering.

[5] Literally, they should 'consider the circle', which signifies the sufi ritual of serving in a circular fashion, from right to left.

[6] *sufri:* a cloth spread out on the floor for meals.

God, the Supreme, says ...Remember the grace
and blessings of God (Niʿmatullāh) upon you:
you were stubborn enemies and He joined your hearts
in love, so that by His grace and blessings,
brothers and sisters you have become. (3:103)

The Path